the new
Bread
Machine book

Marjie Lambert

the new Bread Machine book

Delicious and nourishing breads to home-bake,
at the touch of a switch

APPLE

DEDICATION
Dedicated to my grandmothers, Genevieve Lambert and Letty Belden, who have always
believed in me. And with thanks to Lola, whose herb bread was an inspiration for so
much; to Diana at Quintet; and as always, to Terry.

A QUINTET BOOK

Published by Apple Press
6 Blundell Street
London N7 9BH

ISBN 1-84092-206-0

Reprinted 2000, 2001

This book was designed and produced by
Quintet Publishing Limited
6 Blundell Street
London N7 9BH

Creative Director: Richard Dewing
Designer: Ian Hunt, Linda Henley
Managing Editor: Diana Steedman
Editor: Nicole Foster
Home Economists: Eliza Baird, Jenny Stacey
Photography: Howard Shooter

Typeset in Great Britain by Central Southern Typesetters, Eastbourne
Manufactured in Hong Kong by Regent Publishing Services Ltd
Printed in Singapore by Star Standard Industries (Pte) Ltd

The recipes contained in this book have been compiled for general use in a variety
of machines. Oster, Welbilt and Team breadmakers have been used to test the
recipes. For best results, always refer to your manufacturer's instructions regarding
the proportions of ingredients, especially flour to water. You may need to adjust
these recipes accordingly.

The publishers would like to thank Ceri Hilton-Jones of Team International who
kindly loaned Team Breadmakers for use in testing and photography. The Team
Breadmaker is available from good cookshops and appliance suppliers, and you can
contact Team International at 44-121 328 1998 or via the internet on
http://www.teamuki.com.

CONTENTS

INTRODUCTION
6

TROUBLESHOOTING
16

BASIC BREADS
18

GRAIN BREADS
29

RYE BREADS
43

SOURDOUGH BREADS
53

FRUIT AND VEGETABLE BREADS
66

SWEET BREADS
85

OVEN-BAKED BREADS
100

BREADSTICKS, ROLLS
AND QUICKBREADS
111

HOLIDAY BREADS
119

INDEX
128

INTRODUCTION

Watching a simple loaf of bread rise is almost magical. Who can resist peeping into the bread machine to see the dough rising, forming a perfect dome that will become golden crust and fill the room with tantalizing fragrances? As yeast turns a lump of dough into a crusty sourdough or feather-light rolls, it is easy to be intimidated, to believe that making bread is a trick that only the most experienced cooks should attempt.

In fact, a bread machine makes bread-baking one of the kitchen's easiest tasks. It frees the cook from worries about whether the yeast has been properly proofed and the dough properly kneaded. A novice can measure ingredients into the bread tin, press the Start button and several hours later, with no additional work, have a perfect loaf of hot bread. Later, after gaining confidence, he or she can experiment with plaited loaves and oven-baked rolls.

In an era when most people work full-time and few of us have the time or energy for cooking – especially on weekdays – home-made bread can turn a simple meal into something special. Imagine what a fresh loaf of dark pumpernickel bread will add to soup, or how Southern Feather Rolls will dress up an easy salad. And think how special breakfast would be if the toast were made from a multi-grain bread fresh from the bread machine. As great an invention as the bread machine is, it is almost matched by the bread machine timer that allows us to measure ingredients in the morning for bread that finishes baking just as we get home from work, or that wakes us up first thing with the yeasty fragrance of hot bread.

The bread machine allows you to make a variety of breads to suit your own tastes, adding fruit to a multi-grain bread, spice to a rye bread, onions to sourdough. Hate raisins? Substitute apricots in a recipe – or leave the fruit out altogether. Tired of the uniform texture of white bread? Add wheat germ, oatmeal or bran cereal.

For those of us who enjoy making bread by hand, who like the sensuality of kneading and shaping dough, the bread machine allows us to have home-made bread on other days as well, on days when we can't set aside the time for long periods of kneading and monitoring the rising of dough.

With all that said, understand that the bread machine can be stubborn and some breads temperamental. Most are inflexible in their cycles and won't allow you to shave off a few minutes of kneading or to add more time for a low-rising dough. They will purée fruit and grind down nuts that are added at the beginning of the kneading cycle. And their baking cycles have no tolerance for doughs that are high in sugar or liquid – those can be started in the bread machine but must be baked in a conventional oven.

But even at its inflexible worst, the bread machine will knead the dough for you and put it through its first rising before letting you take over and bake your brioche or babka, rich in butter and eggs, in the oven.

You can still enjoy kneading the dough before its second rising, incorporating fruit, nuts or cheese that would have been shredded to bits in the bread machine. With oven-baked bread, you also have the choice of shaping the loaf into a round, a plait or a baguette or baking it in a loaf tin. You can paint the dough with an egg wash that will produce a shiny crust, or you can garnish the top with nuts, grains, seeds or sugar.

GETTING TO KNOW YOUR BREAD MACHINE

Like a car, a computer or any other piece of equipment, every bread machine has its idiosyncrasies. Each brand is different, and many brands make several models. Some warm the ingredients before kneading them. Some suggest you add liquid ingredients first, others dry ingredients. Some are noisier than others and will wake you long before your alarm clock – if you set the timer to bake bread overnight. Some give you more choices and settings – do you want that wholewheat bread with a light, medium or dark crust?

To get accustomed to a new machine – and this book – start with a simple recipe, such as white, honey wheat, potato or egg bread. Watch the elasticity of the dough during kneading and see how it comes out, then consult Troubleshooting on pages 16–17 for help in adjusting the recipe.

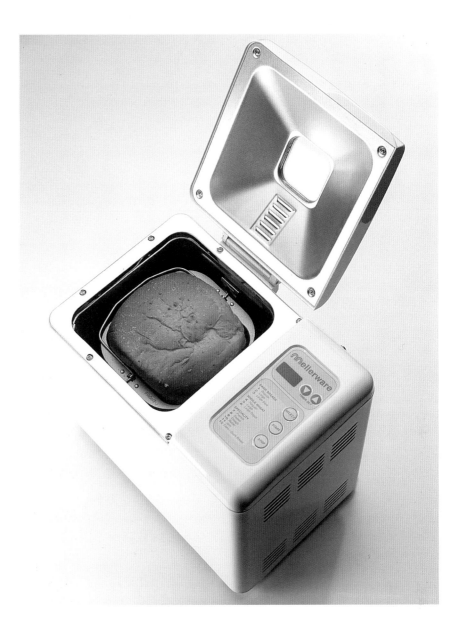

Choose a machine that offers different settings for different types of bread – from a dense pumpernickel to featherlight white bread.

Get accustomed to your bread machine's parts, controls and timings, by starting with a simple recipe such as those on pages 19 and 22.

BAKING BREAD

Before you begin, read the recipe. Make sure you have time for any advance preparation such as boiling potatoes or mixing a sponge for sourdough. Assemble all the ingredients before starting. Most ingredients are best when used at room temperature, though some bread machines warm the ingredients before mixing them. Cold liquids and butter can be warmed in the microwave if necessary. Eggs can be placed in a bowl of warm water. Frozen yeast should be brought to room temperature, but yeast that has been kept in the refrigerator will warm up quickly enough. Although yeast dough may rise faster with a boost from the microwave, never put unmixed yeast in the microwave to warm it.

Be sure the paddle is properly seated in the bottom of the bread tin. Add the ingredients to the bread tin in the order suggested by your bread machine instructions. This may vary from one machine to the next. If there are no instructions, add liquids first, then dry ingredients. Yeast should be added last and should not be in direct contact with unmixed salt or wheat germ. If you are using the timer or if the bread machine warms ingredients before mixing them, make a small well in the flour and put

the yeast there so it does not come into contact with liquids before mixing. Fit the bread tin securely into the machine.

Select settings on the control panel according to the manufacturer's instructions. The more modern bread machines generally have more choices, but the basic differences between the settings are these: wholewheat bread rises more slowly than bread made with white flour; sweet breads must be cooked at a lower setting or they will scorch; the French bread setting makes a crustier bread, but that may make it more difficult to remove from the bread tin. Experiment with the light, medium and dark settings to determine your own taste. Often, sweet breads will need the light-crust setting to avoid scorching.

If you are using the timer, do not use recipes that require eggs or other highly perishable ingredients if there will be a delay of more than an hour. I have not had trouble using small quantities of butter or milk that must be left overnight. However, you may wish to substitute vegetable oil for butter. You can substitute water and powdered milk for whole milk when using the timer. Use 3 tablespoons of dry milk per 250 ml (8 fl oz) of water. Be sure to layer liquids first, then dry ingredients, with the powdered milk added after the flour so it does not mix with the water prematurely.

Check the dough while the bread machine is kneading it. Soon you will be able to recognize when more flour or liquid is needed. The dough should be smooth, slightly tacky to the touch and slump just slightly when the paddle stops. If the dough is stiff and the paddle leaves ragged edges, add liquid one teaspoon at a time. If there's a sticky layer of dough on the bottom of the pan while most of it is being kneaded or the dough is so soft that it collapses when the paddle stops, add a tablespoon of flour or more. Be aware that some recipes call for a very soft dough; most of these will be oven-baked. Also, be aware that some cereals such as oatmeal and bran will absorb extra liquid as they bake.

Don't be shy about lifting the lid and watching the kneading process. It is only when the bread is in the rising and baking stages that an open lid will interfere with temperature controls. And even then it's all right to peep as long as you do it quickly!

When the bread is done, remove it from the machine and the bread tin immediately. Although a few machines now have additional controls to prevent this, in most machines the steam released by the bread will condense in the pan, making the bread rubbery or soggy on the outside. The bread should cool for at least 30 minutes before you cut into it.

The kneading paddle should be well-seated in the bottom of the tin.

Add ingredients in the order suggested by the manufacturer.

The tin should sit securely inside the machine.

ADDITIONS

Fruit, vegetables and nuts added at the beginning of the kneading cycle will be puréed or shredded into tiny pieces. Sometimes this is the desired result, but usually it is not. If you want the raisins to remain whole and the walnuts to remain in chunks, add them 10 to 15 minutes into the kneading cycle. Most bread machines have a buzzer that sounds when it is time to add the additions. (Unfortunately, most don't allow you to cancel the buzzer when you don't need it.)

If you are using the timer to make the bread and don't have any choice but to add all the ingredients at the beginning, you need to take into account whether any juicy additions such as still-moist dried apricots, sun-dried tomatoes or roasted red peppers will release extra liquid into the dough if they are puréed. Some can add as much as one or two tablespoons of liquid. If that is the case, you will want to add an extra tablespoon or so of flour to the mixture.

Some sweet breads with sugary additions may not do well if baked with a timer. Too much sugar can cause bread to scorch or become sticky. Candied fruit that is added at the beginning of the kneading cycle instead of at the fruit buzzer may be shredded and consequently release too much sugar into the dough.

USING THE TIMER

If you are using the bread machine timer so that the mixing will be delayed, the ingredients should be layered so that the yeast does not come into contact with the liquid ingredients prematurely. Consult your bread machine instructions for advice – the procedure may vary from one brand to the next, and a few models hold the yeast separate and release it at the proper time. But in general, when using a timer, the liquids should be put in the bread tin first, followed by the dry ingredients and finally the yeast. Yeast should not come into prolonged contact with any concentration of salt, oat bran or wheat germ, which may interfere with the yeast's rising action.

Recipes using eggs, cottage cheese or other highly perishable ingredients should not be made with a timer if there will be a delay of more than one hour or so. See Baking Bread, page 8, for notes on substituting powdered milk for whole milk.

LEFT Consider the moisture content of fruit or nut additions. Roasted peppers or juicy pears will increase the liquid and sugar balance.

OVEN-BAKED BREADS

Any of the breads in this book can be baked in a conventional oven. Remove the dough from the bread machine after the first rising, punch down on a lightly floured surface, and knead lightly. Shape the dough into a loaf or rolls and place in a baking tin or on a sheet. Cover lightly and let rise in a warm place, remembering that wholewheat and low-gluten doughs require more rising time than doughs made with white flour. Baking times and temperatures vary, but most loaves should be baked at 180°C/350°F/Gas 4 or 190°C/375°F/ Gas 5 for 30 to 35 minutes, a little longer for the 675 g (1½ lb) loaves.

I use a 24 cm (9½ in) loaf tin for most breads. The 675 g (1½ lb) breads made with 100 percent bread flour may need a larger tin. The 450 g (1 lb) loaves that include rye or other low-gluten flours will rise higher and look more attractive in a 20 cm (8 in) tin.

A cautionary note about bread tins and baking sheets: the materials, construction and finishes vary widely and will affect the baking time and temperature. Double-layered tins with an insulating air cushion protect against scorching, and are especially useful with sweet breads, but breads baked in these tins will take longer to bake. Some of the heavy, expensive tins with black surfaces will brown the bread faster. If a dark, crusty exterior is not desirable, you will need to lower the baking temperature and/or reduce the baking time. If you use a glass loaf tin, reduce the oven temperature by 4°C/25°F/Gas ½.

BREAD-BAKING INGREDIENTS

YEAST

The first yeasts known to have been used were wild yeasts unintentionally captured from the air when dough was left standing for hours and puffed up. That was the first sourdough, and it was baked by Egyptians about 4000 BC. Before that, bread was unleavened, made of meal ground from corn and mixed with water.

Sprinkle a little flour on a clean, smooth surface and knead gently.

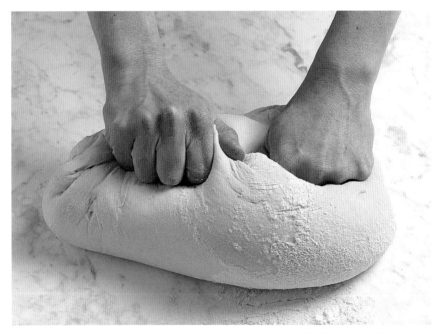

Notice the elasticity developing. The dough is neither crumbly dry nor sticky.

Later, bakers discovered a yeasty byproduct of beer-brewing that acted as a leavening agent in bread without leaving a sour taste. It was not until the 19th century that compressed yeast was perfected. Now, we have our choice of fresh yeast, active dry yeast and rapid-rise yeast. All the recipes in this book call for active dry yeast. The active dry yeast in little envelopes is perfectly

acceptable, but I find bread rises higher and more consistently with bread machine yeast, available in 100 g (4 oz) jars. This yeast keeps longer if stored in the refrigerator. If your bread machine has a rapid-rise cycle, rapid-rise yeast can be used, but bread made with rapid-rise yeast rises less than other yeasts, and will rise very little when it is used in a wholewheat bread.

Activated by water and fed by sugar, yeast ferments. This is why virtually all bread recipes, even for breads that are not sweet, contain a small amount of sugar. The fermentation creates tiny bubbles of carbon dioxide gas that make the dough rise. Gluten, an elastic protein in the dough, allows the dough to stretch and holds in the gas bubbles. Once the yeast reaches a certain temperature during baking, it dies and the fermentation stops. But by then, the bubbles have been captured by the gluten. The more gluten in the flour, the higher the bread will rise.

FLOUR

Many flours are available, including barley, millet, oat, corn and rice flour. Some flours have been milled for thousands of years. But only wheat and rye flours have the gluten necessary to make leavened bread. The other flours can be used in combination with wheat and rye flours, adding different tastes and textures.

WHEAT FLOURS Wheat flours are milled from the wheat berry. The berry consists of three parts: the outer hull, or bran; the small germ or embryo inside; and the endosperm, a starchy material that feeds the embryo.

White flour, including plain flour and bread flour, consists of the milled endosperm with the bran and germ removed. Plain flour is milled to be used in a variety of ways and is made with a combination of hard and soft wheats. Bread flour, milled specifically for bread, has a higher gluten content and will absorb more liquid. It is made only from hard wheat. Because of the higher gluten content, breads made with bread flour will rise higher than breads made with plain flour. The recipes in this book were tested with bread flour, but all can be made with plain flour.

Wholewheat flour contains the bran and the germ of the wheat berry, as well as the endosperm. It has less gluten than white flour, so it rises more slowly and not as high. It also may have a

slightly bitter flavour. Most wholewheat breads are made with a combination of wholewheat and white flours.

Graham flour is a coarsely ground wholewheat flour milled from soft winter wheat. It has less gluten than ordinary wholewheat flour. It adds texture and a slightly chewier character to bread. The quality of graham flour varies widely. Some manufacturers have begun labelling ordinary wholewheat flour as graham flour; others package inferior flour with wheat bran and label it graham flour. Your best bet is to buy graham flour from a reputable health-food shop or mail-order baking supply catalogue (see listing on page 128).

Semolina flour is a high-gluten white flour milled from durum or hard winter wheat, with only the bran layer removed. Although its main use is in pasta, it makes a delicious bread when used in combination with other flours and adds crustiness.

Wheat gluten or vital wheat gluten flour is a high-protein, hard-wheat flour from which most of the starch has been removed. This flour makes a useful addition to bread made with gluten-free or low-gluten flours, such as rye, since it will give dough more elasticity and make bread rise higher. Add one tablespoon of gluten flour for every 130 g (5 oz) of low-gluten flour. Gluten flour is available in health-food and specialist shops or through mail-order companies (see listing on page 128).

RYE FLOURS Rye is a hardy grain that grows well in cold, wet climates where wheat does not, which explains why rye flour is so common in Scandinavian and Russian breads. Although it contains gluten, it does not have as much as wheat flours. Breads made with only rye flour are heavy and compact. Most rye breads are made with a combination of rye and wheat flours.

Medium or light rye flour, the most common rye flour available, is milled only from the endosperm. Dark rye and pumpernickel, which are difficult to find except through baking supply mail-order catalogues, are milled from the bran, germ and endosperm of the rye berry. They are darker, coarser flours that add texture and flavour to bread.

OTHER FLOURS Non-wheat flours are low in gluten or are gluten free. They should be used in combination with wheat or rye flours unless you require entirely gluten-free breads for health reasons.

Amaranth flour, a staple of the Aztec people, has a nutty, slightly spicy flavour. It is high in protein but very low in gluten.

Barley flour, milled from a grain that dates back to the Stone Age, has a slightly sweet taste, a soft texture and a low gluten content. Used in quantity, it makes bread sticky; some people recommend using it in combination with millet flour, which seems to counteract the stickiness.

Buckwheat flour, made from the seeds of a cereal grass, adds a pungent, earthy flavour to bread. It is a high-fat flour, low in gluten.

Corn flour, milled from the whole kernel of corn, adds a sweet flavour to bread. It has no gluten. Corn starch and cornflour are milled only from the endosperm.

Millet, a staple food in parts of Africa and Asia, adds a pleasantly gritty texture to bread. It is low in gluten.

Oat flour, made from oats that have been ground into powder, is very low in gluten but high in protein.

Potato flour, milled from the whole potato, is gluten-free. In bread-making, it is usually used in small quantities to lighten heavy loaves.

Quinoa flour, an ancient pearly grain flour from Peru, gives bread a nutty flavour. It is high in protein and has the health benefit of being gluten-free.

Rice flour, the flour most commonly used in gluten-free breads, is milled

The higher the level of gluten in the flour you choose, the better the loaf texture.

from white or brown rice. It makes bread with a sweet flavour and chewy texture. Rice flour made from white rice has the husk, germ and bran removed; brown rice flour includes the bran.

Soybean flour gives bread a moist texture, is high in protein and gluten-free. It adds a slight bitter flavour.

GRAINS

Grains can add flavour, texture and protein to bread. Typically they are added in small quantities, 2 to 4 tablespoons for a 450 g (1 lb) loaf. They do not contribute to rising and are not a substitute for flour. Some grains, particularly those eaten as cereals such as oat bran and wheat germ, can be found in well-stocked supermarkets. Most are available in health-food shops.

WHEAT Many forms of wheat are available as grains. The wheat berry is the whole grain and is much too hard to eat as is. It can be softened by sprouting

– the berry is soaked in water that is changed at least twice a day for several days – or by boiling with lots of water for at least one hour.

Cracked wheat is the wheat berry that has been broken into pieces. It is still too hard to eat without prior cooking, but it can be softened by boiling for 30 to 40 minutes.

Bulgur is a wheat berry that has been steamed and cracked. It adds crunch to bread. It can be added as it is to bread in small quantities, or boiled for 6 minutes and drained.

Wheat bran, the outer hull of the grain, is also known as miller's bran or unprocessed bran flakes. It interferes with the elasticity of gluten and should be used in small quantities.

Wheat germ is the embryo of the wheat berry. It is high in nutrients, has a nutty flavour and is high in oils that can turn rancid if it is not kept refrigerated. Wheat germ can be bought already toasted, which enhances its flavour.

Bran cereals, such as bran flakes or All-Bran, are made with wheat bran and other ingredients, including sugar and salt, and may be toasted. They add good flavour and texture to bread.

OTHER GRAINS Cornmeal, milled from corn, adds a sweet flavour and, if uncooked, a crumbly texture. It can interfere with the gluten, so use it in small quantities, or cook or soften it in boiling water before adding to dough.

Millet, widely used as birdseed, adds crunch to bread when it is added in its whole, unhulled state.

Oatmeal, the most nutritious of the cereal grasses, means old-fashioned rolled oats in this cookbook. The husk is removed and the grain is sliced, steamed and rolled. The dried oats may have trouble absorbing thicker liquids such as applesauce or buttermilk, so may be soaked briefly in boiling water before being added to other ingredients.

Oat bran is the hull of the oat and is high in soluble fibre. Oat bran can interfere with the gluten in bread dough and should be used in small quantities.

Rye berries, much like wheat berries, are the whole grain and must be boiled for an hour or so to make them soft enough to eat.

Cereals, seeds and bulghur wheat give mellow flavours to wholesome breads.

SALT

Salt is critical in bread. In addition to enhancing the flavour, it strengthens the gluten. Salt-free bread may rise nicely, but it will collapse. However, salt in high concentrations will inhibit the yeast's rising action. Salt and yeast should be added so that they do not come in contact with each other before the dough is mixed. Because some sodium is necessary for bread to rise and hold its shape, most salt substitutes cannot be used.

SWEETENERS

Yeast ferments best when it feeds on sugar in some form. Sugar also acts as a preservative. It caramelizes during

baking and contributes to the golden colour of the crust. But too much sugar will interfere with the yeast's rising action and cause the bread to collapse. Most yeast breads and rolls are not very sweet. Dessert breads get their sweetness from a glaze, dry sugar topping, or another addition made after baking.

Sugar scorches easily. Many machines have a setting for sweet breads and bake them at a lower temperature or for shorter times. If your bread machine does not have a sweet-bread setting, chose the light-crust option.

The addition of candied fruits is a particular problem with bread machines. When candied fruit is used, it is usually in breads that already have several tablespoons of sweetener. The kneading shreds the candied fruit and releases more sugar into the dough. Candied fruit should be added late in the kneading cycle, or kneaded in by hand after the first rising if the bread is to be baked in the oven.

Sugar and brown sugar can always be substituted for each other. Icing sugar contains cornflour and should not be used as a substitute. In small quantities – 1 or 2 tablespoons – sugar, honey and molasses can be substituted for each other in equal amounts. Tablespoon for tablespoon, most honeys are slightly sweeter than sugar. When the recipe calls for more than two tablespoons of sweetener, substitute two parts honey for three parts sugar; e.g., 2 tablespoons of honey for 3 tablespoons of sugar. Molasses is not as sweet as sugar. When substituting more than 2 tablespoons, use 4 tablespoons of molasses for 3 tablespoons of sugar. Maple syrup can be substituted in equal amounts for sugar.

Liquid sweeteners, including honey, molasses and maple syrup, should be counted towards the total liquid contents of the ingredients. A change of one tablespoon probably won't make a difference, but larger substitutions of a liquid sweetener for sugar or vice versa will. Watch the dough as it kneads, and adjust liquid or flour as needed.

Sweeteners act to stimulate the yeast, and contribute to the golden crust.

LIQUID

The variety of liquids used in bread-baking is nearly infinite. Most common are water, milk, buttermilk and eggs, but beer, wine, orange juice and the water that potatoes are boiled in are not unusual additions. Soured cream, yoghurt, cottage cheese, ricotta cheese, mashed potatoes, apple sauce, pumpkin and other puréed fruits and vegetables also contribute liquid; often half their volume is liquid.

A bread made with water as its only liquid ingredient will have a crisper crust. Milk gives it a softer crust and more golden colour. You can substitute equal amounts of whole, skimmed and non-fat milk for each other. Powdered milk is very helpful in bread-baking, particularly when the bread is being baked on a timer and the ingredients will be sitting at room temperature for hours. Use 3 tablespoons of powdered milk per cup of liquid, and layer so it does not come in contact with liquids before it is mixed. Powdered milk is also used when the recipe calls for another liquid, such as eggs or mashed potatoes, but you still want a golden colour or softer crust.

Large eggs are recommended for all the recipes.

Buttermilk gives bread a tender crumb and a hint of tangy flavour. It also adds acidity to the dough that is usually neutralized with a pinch of baking soda.

EGGS

Eggs give bread a softer crust and richer flavour and contribute to the leavening. Recipes were tested for this cookbook with large eggs, which equal 50 ml (2 fl oz) of liquid. You can also use pasteurized egg substitutes. Breads containing eggs should not be made with a timer if the ingredients stand for more than an hour before being kneaded.

FATS

Fats are used sparingly in most breads but are important in small quantities because they act as preservatives and add a tender texture. A true French bread uses no fat and goes stale in less than 24 hours. Butter, margarine, vegetable oil, shortening and lard can be used interchangeably. In small quantities there will be no noticeable difference. If you are substituting more than one tablespoon of a liquid fat for a solid fat or vice versa, the amount of other liquid in the dough will have to be adjusted.

Lard gives bread a slightly flakier texture and crustier finish. I don't like to use margarine because it can contain water. If you're watching cholesterol and want a substitute for butter, use vegetable oil. You can substitute olive oil, but in quantities less than three tablespoons (in a 450 g/1 lb loaf), you are not likely to notice a difference in taste. Speciality oils such as walnut or sesame oil are strongly flavoured and should be used sparingly.

If you want to cut every bit of fat out of your bread, you can substitute apple sauce or puréed prunes. Puréed fruit contains some liquid, so the amount of other liquids in the bread may have to be adjusted.

Butter should always be brought to room temperature before the dough is kneaded, because soft butter mixes more readily. This is especially critical in high-fat breads such as brioche.

A note about greasing baking tins or sheets: use butter, solid vegetable shortening or a spray. Oil will soak into the dough, and margarines may scorch.

BELOW Sit back and enjoy the rewards: great bread baked fresh every day.

TOO MUCH OR TOO LITTLE LIQUID

The most frequent cause of trouble with bread made in a bread machine is too much or too little liquid. Keep in mind that flour absorbs moisture from the air. That's why a loaf of bread may turn out perfect one time and awful the next. In humid weather, the flour may have already absorbed an extra 1 or 2 tablespoons of moisture. If you add the usual amount of liquid, it may mushroom and collapse, or develop a coarse, holey texture. Likewise, if the climate is very dry, the flour may need a little extra moisture, or it will have a dense, heavy texture or a gnarled top.

Check the dough about 10 minutes into the kneading cycle. The dough should be smooth, soft and slightly tacky. It should settle just the slightest bit, but hold its shape when the kneading paddle stops. If the dough is very soft, settles quickly when the kneading paddle stops and can't hold its shape, add 1 tablespoon of flour. If the dough is stiff with ragged edges and imprints of the paddle remain in the dough for more than a couple of seconds, add 1 tablespoon of liquid.

TEMPERATURE

Ingredients should be at room temperature. But "room temperature" may be too hot or too cold in particularly hot or cold weather. If the ingredients are too cold, they may not activate the yeast soon enough. If they are too warm – such as on a hot day in a kitchen that is not air-conditioned – the yeast may cause the dough to rise too much and overflow the machine.

ADDING FRUIT AND VEGETABLES

Another variable that can put too much liquid into the dough is fruit or vegetables. If fruit or vegetables are added at the beginning of the kneading cycle, they will be ground up and release more liquid than if they were added at the beeper or after the first kneading. If you're using the timer to knead the bread, have to add fruit or vegetables at the beginning and can't check the dough during the kneading, reduce liquids by 1 to 2 teaspoons for drier additions like raisins or sun-dried tomatoes, and by 1 to 2 tablespoons for wetter additions, like shredded apple or roasted red peppers.

PROBLEMS AND ANSWERS

BREAD COLLAPSED

- *Too much liquid.* Next time reduce liquid by 2 tablespoons, then monitor the dough as it kneads and adjust liquid or flour for a firm but sticky dough.
- *You omitted the salt or used a salt substitute.* The gluten needs some salt to support it as it rises. Minimum amount is ½ teaspoon for a 450 g (1 lb) loaf, ¾ teaspoon for a 675 g (1½ lb) loaf. Most salt substitutes will not work in supporting the gluten.
- *Too much sugar.* Decrease by 1 tablespoon next time. You're getting into dangerous territory with more than 40 g (1½ oz) sugar for a 450 g (1 lb) loaf, 6 tablespoons for a 675 g (1½ lb) loaf, although some recipes will work with more. Don't forget that sugary additions like candied fruit increase the quantity of sugar.

BREAD HAS BURNED CRUST, BUT CENTRE IS FINE

- *Too much sugar can cause the crust to burn.* Set controls for sweet bread and/or light crust. If it still burns – or your machine does not have those settings – reduce sugar by 1 tablespoon. Or remove the bread 5 minutes before the machine is done. Or bake the bread in a loaf tin in a conventional oven.

BREAD NOT BAKED IN CENTRE

- *Too much liquid or not enough flour.* Next time, reduce liquid by 1 to 2 tablespoons or increase flour by 2 to 4 tablespoons (if the bread tin has room for a larger loaf); then monitor dough as it kneads, and adjust flour or liquid for a firm but sticky dough. The bread machine has little tolerance for dough that varies much from a set ratio of liquid to flour. Often, those same breads – especially sweet breads like kugelhopf or panettone – will turn out fine when baked in a conventional oven. Set the bread machine to make dough, then remove it, punch it down and put it in a buttered loaf pan. Let it rise in a warm place for 45 minutes to 1 hour, then bake at 190°F/375°F/Gas 5 for about 30 minutes.
- *If it is a sweet bread* and has sticky pockets, reduce the sugar or sweetener by 1 tablespoon.

BREAD HAS GNARLED TOP AND/OR HEAVY, DENSE TEXTURE

- *Not enough liquid or too much flour.* If the bread tin has room for a larger loaf, add 1 to 2 tablespoons of liquid next time; otherwise, reduce flour by 2 to 4 tablespoons. Monitor dough as it kneads and adjust liquid or flour for a firm but sticky texture. (Note: If you tap the measuring cup several times to get flour to settle, you may be cramming too much flour into the measuring cup.)
- *Too much low-gluten flour.* Breads that consist entirely of rye or, to a lesser extent, wholewheat flour will be dense and heavy. Sometimes, this is desirable. If it is not, substitute bread flour for part of the rye or wholewheat flour. Or add wheat gluten, an additive available at health-food shops.
- *Too many extras, such as oatmeal, wheat germ, fruit or nuts substituted for flour.* If there is room in your bread tin, add 3 to 4 tablespoons bread flour and about 2 tablespoons of liquid. Otherwise, reduce the extras.

BREAD HAS MUSHROOM TOP WITH AIR UNDERNEATH, OR HAS TUNNELS OR COARSE HOLEY TEXTURE

- *Too much liquid.* Next time, reduce the amount of liquid by 1 to 2 tablespoons, then monitor the dough as it kneads and adjust the amount of liquid or flour for a firm but sticky dough.
- *Too much yeast.* Reduce yeast by $\frac{1}{4}$ teaspoon for a smaller loaf, $\frac{1}{2}$ teaspoon for a larger loaf.

BREAD RISES TOO MUCH

- *Too much yeast.* Reduce the amount of yeast by $\frac{1}{2}$ teaspoon next time.
- *Too much liquid, especially if there are large air pockets in bread.* Reduce liquid by 1 to 2 tablespoons next time, check kneading, and adjust flour for firm, sticky texture.

BREAD DOESN'T RISE ENOUGH

- *Not enough yeast.* Increase yeast by $\frac{1}{2}$ teaspoon.
- *Yeast is not fresh.* Proof by putting 2 teaspoons of yeast in 125 ml (4 fl oz) warm water 40.5 to 46°C (105 to 115°F). If it does not develop a thick head of foam in 5 to 10 minutes, discard the yeast.
- *You're using rapid-rise yeast or the rapid-rise cycle.* The price for this shortcut is a loaf that doesn't rise as high. (See note on Yeast on page 10.)
- *You're using yeast that does not do well in bread machines.* Switch to yeast produced specifically for bread machines. (See note on Yeast on page 10.)
- *You used hot liquid* – over 46°C (115°F) – and it killed the yeast.
- *Not enough liquid.* Increase liquid by 1 tablespoon next time.
- *Too much sugar* (honey, molasses, etc.) may be interfering with yeast. If it is a high-sugar bread (or if it has sugary additions like candied fruit), reduce sugar by 1 tablespoon, or increase yeast by $\frac{1}{4}$ teaspoon. Conversely, yeast works better when there is at least 1 teaspoon of sugar to feed it. Although some recipes, such as French Bread, get along without it, the yeast rises better with a small amount of sweetener.
- *You're using too much low-gluten flour.* Increase the proportion of white flour. Or substitute bread flour for plain flour.
- *Your tap water is too hard* (alkaline). Add 1 teaspoon of lemon juice or vinegar.
- *Too much salt.* This may be because you added salty extras, like salted nuts, without reducing the amount of salt.
- *You allowed the salt and yeast to come in contact with each other prior to mixing.* A high proportion of salt in direct contact with yeast can kill the yeast.
- *You opened the lid during the rising stage and allowed warm air to escape.*

BREAD DOESN'T RISE AT ALL AND IS A STICKY OR BURNT LAYERED MESS

- *You forgot to set the paddle in the pan, or it was not firmly seated and came loose.*

BASIC BREADS

White Bread 19

Rich White Bread 19

Wholewheat Bread 20

Jon's Polentaporter Bread 20

Soured Cream Spice Bread 21

Herbed Cottage Cheese
Bread 22

Potato Bread 22

Soured Cream Wholewheat
Bread with Herbs 24

Dill Onion Yoghurt Bread 25

Kathy's Pepper Cheese
Bread 27

Walnut Ricotta
Wholewheat Bread 27

Buttermilk Chive Bread 28

White Bread

This is an all-purpose white bread.

450 g (1 lb) LOAF	INGREDIENTS	675 g (1½ lb) LOAF	METHOD
120 ml (4 fl oz)	water	175 ml (6 fl oz)	Put ingredients in bread tin in order suggested by your bread machine instructions. Set for white bread, medium crust. Press Start.
50 ml (2 fl oz)	milk	6 tbsp	
1 tbsp	butter	1½ tbsp	
1 tbsp	sugar	1½ tbsp	
1 tsp	salt	1½ tsp	
270 g (10 oz)	bread flour	425 g (15 oz)	
1½ tsp	yeast	2¼ tsp	

Rich White Bread

Using egg for part of your liquid ingredients gives bread a little more richness and colour.

450 g (1 lb) LOAF	INGREDIENTS	675 g (1½ lb) LOAF	METHOD
4 tbsp	water	6 tbsp	Put ingredients in bread tin in order suggested by your bread machine instructions. Set for white bread, medium crust. Press Start.
50 ml (2 fl oz)	milk	50 ml (2 fl oz)	
1	egg	2	
1 tbsp	butter	1½ tbsp	
1 tbsp	honey	1½ tbsp	
1 tsp	salt	1½ tsp	
270 g (10 oz)	bread flour	425 g (15 oz)	
1½ tsp	yeast	2¼ tsp	

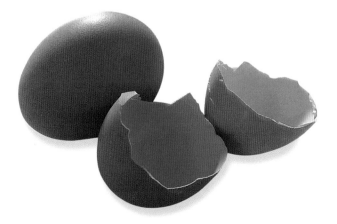

WHOLEWHEAT BREAD

This is a basic honey and wheat bread, made with equal parts white and wholewheat flour so it will not be too dense.

450 g (1 lb) LOAF	INGREDIENTS	675 g (1½ lb) LOAF	METHOD
120 ml (4 fl oz)	water	175 ml (6 fl oz)	Put ingredients in bread tin in order suggested by your bread machine instructions. Set for wholewheat bread, medium crust. Press Start.
50 ml (2 fl oz)	milk	6 tbsp	
1 tbsp	butter	1½ tbsp	
1 tbsp	honey	1½ tbsp	
1 tsp	salt	1½ tsp	
130 g (5 oz)	wholewheat flour	200 g (7½ oz)	
130 g (5 oz)	bread flour	200 g (7½ oz)	
1½ tsp	yeast	2¼ tsp	

JON'S POLENTAPORTER BREAD

This bread is a creation of my friend Jon Engellenner, whose hobby is making beer for drinking and cooking. He recommends eating this bread warm, with cool-weather dishes like chilli, soups and stews. Here is his description: This easy recipe produces a bold and dense brown bread with overtones of grain and nuts. The polenta provides a little crunch; the sesame seeds give a nut-like flavour. One way to adjust its character is to substitute stout for the porter. Stout, the Cabernet Sauvignon of beers, sits a notch above porter on the darkness/density scale. Using stout increases the complexity, maltiness and even, just slightly, the bitterness of the bread. Beware: this variation is not for light-beer drinkers.

450 g (1 lb) LOAF	INGREDIENTS	675 g (1½ lb) LOAF	METHOD
200 ml (7½ fl oz)	porter ale or stout	330 ml (10½ fl oz)	Put all ingredients except sesame seeds in bread tin in order suggested by your bread machine instructions. Set for white bread, medium crust. Press Start. After about 15 minutes or when the beeper signals time to add fruit, add sesame seeds.
1 tbsp	groundnut oil	1½ tbsp	
1 tsp	light brown sugar, packed	1½ tsp	
¾ tsp	salt	1¼ tsp	
2 tbsp	raw polenta	3 tbsp	
270 g (10 oz)	bread flour	425 g (15 oz)	
1 tsp	yeast	1½ tsp	
1 tbsp	sesame seeds	1½ tbsp	

SOURED CREAM SPICE BREAD

This bread makes delicious toast.

450 g (1 lb) LOAF	INGREDIENTS	675 g (1 ½ lb) LOAF
120 ml (4 fl oz)	water	175 ml (6 fl oz)
120 ml (4 fl oz)	soured cream	175 ml (6 fl oz)
2 tbsp	butter	3 tbsp
1 tbsp	honey	1 ½ tbsp
1 tsp	cinnamon	1 ½ tsp
1 tsp	ground ginger	1 ½ tsp
½ tsp	ground allspice	¾ tsp
1 tsp	salt	1 ½ tsp
300 g (12 oz)	bread flour	550 g (1 ½ lb)
1 ½ tsp	yeast	2 ¼ tsp

METHOD

Put ingredients in bread tin in order suggested by your bread machine instructions. Set for white bread, medium crust. Press Start.

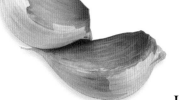

HERBED COTTAGE CHEESE BREAD

This savoury white bread is lightened by egg and cottage cheese. It goes well with meals and in sandwiches. You may need to adjust the amount of water slightly, depending on the water content of the cottage cheese.

450 g (1 lb) LOAF	INGREDIENTS	675 g (1½ lb) LOAF
130 g (5½ oz)	cottage cheese	200 g (8 oz)
1	egg	1 + 1 yolk
3 tbsp	water	4½ tbsp
1 tbsp	butter	1½ tbsp
1 tbsp	sugar	1½ tbsp
1 tsp	salt	1½ tsp
1	clove garlic, pressed or crushed	2
1 tsp	dried basil	1½ tsp
1 tsp	dried oregano	1½ tsp
¼ tsp	dried thyme	½ tsp
¼ tsp	fresh-ground black pepper	½ tsp
270 g (10 oz)	bread flour	425 g (15 oz)
1½ tsp	yeast	2¼ tsp

METHOD

Put ingredients in bread tin in order suggested by your bread machine instructions. Set for white bread, medium crust. Press Start. The stiffness of the dough may vary, depending on the liquid content of the cottage cheese. Watch the dough while it is kneading and add a little flour, 1 tablespoon at a time, if it is too soft. Add water, 1 teaspoon at a time, if the dough is too stiff.

POTATO BREAD

Adding mashed potatoes to bread subtly changes the texture and enriches the flavour. The recipe is based on pure mashed potatoes, with no additions. Instead of milk and water, you can substitute the water the potatoes were cooked in.

450 g (1 lb) LOAF	INGREDIENTS	675 g (1½ lb) LOAF
115 g (4 oz)	mashed potatoes	175 g (6 oz)
50 ml (2 fl oz)	milk	65 ml (2½ fl oz)
3 tbsp	water	65 ml (2½ fl oz)
2 tbsp	vegetable oil	3 tbsp
1 tbsp	honey	1½ tbsp
1 tsp	salt	1½ tsp
295 g (11 oz)	bread flour	425 g (15 oz)
1½ tsp	yeast	2¼ tsp

METHOD

Put ingredients in bread tin in order suggested by your bread machine instructions. Set for white bread, medium crust. Press Start.

RIGHT Herbed Cottage Cheese Bread

SOURED CREAM WHOLEWHEAT BREAD WITH HERBS

This is a light, wholewheat bread, flavoured with rosemary and thyme. Fresh rosemary is preferable, but dried rosemary can be used.

450 g (1 lb) LOAF	INGREDIENTS	675 g (1½ lb) LOAF
1	egg	2
2 tbsp	water	1 tbsp
125 ml (4 fl oz)	soured cream	175 ml (6 fl oz)
1 tbsp	butter	1½ tbsp
1 tbsp	sugar	1½ tbsp
1 tsp	finely chopped rosemary	1½ tsp
½ tsp	dried thyme	¾ tsp
1 tsp	salt	1½ tsp
95 g (3½ oz)	wholewheat flour	130 g (5 oz)
185 g (6½ oz)	bread flour	270 g (10 oz)
1½ tsp	yeast	2¼ tsp

METHOD

Put ingredients in bread tin in order suggested by your bread machine instructions. Set for wholewheat bread, medium crust. Press Start.

DILL ONION YOGHURT BREAD

This white bread has a tender grain, the flavour of onions and dill, and a slight tang added by the yoghurt. It is a good sandwich bread.

450 g (1 lb) LOAF	INGREDIENTS	675 g (1½ lb) LOAF
65 ml (2½ fl oz)	water	120 ml (4 fl oz)
125 ml (4 fl oz)	plain yoghurt	185 ml (6 fl oz)
2 tbsp	butter	3 tbsp
1 tbsp	sugar	1½ tbsp
2 tsp	dried dill weed	1 tbsp
2 tsp	dried onion flakes	1 tbsp
1 tsp	salt	1½ tsp
270 g (10 oz)	bread flour	425 g (15 oz)
1½ tsp	yeast	2¼ tsp

METHOD

Put ingredients in bread tin in order suggested by your bread machine instructions. Set for white bread, medium crust. Press Start.

KATHY'S PEPPER CHEESE BREAD

One of my colleagues, Kathy Trumbull, asked me to help her recreate a favourite bread from years ago. It was a light wheat bread made with black pepper and Parmesan cheese, and she loved to use it for cheese sandwiches. Here it is.

450 g (1 lb) LOAF	INGREDIENTS	675 g (1½ lb) LOAF
175 ml (6 fl oz)	water	250 ml (8 fl oz)
2 tbsp	vegetable oil	3 tbsp
1 tbsp	sugar	1½ tbsp
2 tbsp	powdered milk	3 tbsp
50 g (2 oz)	grated Parmesan cheese	75 g (3 oz)
1½ tsp	freshly ground black pepper	2¼ tsp
1 tsp	salt	1½ tsp
185 g (6½ oz)	bread flour	270 g (10 oz)
95 g (3½ oz)	wholewheat flour	130 g (5 oz)
1½ tsp	yeast	2¼ tsp

METHOD

Put ingredients in bread tin in order suggested by your bread machine instructions. Set for wholewheat bread, medium crust. Press Start.

TIP

If you use freshly grated cheese, pack it tightly or much of the measurement will be air.

WALNUT RICOTTA WHOLEWHEAT BREAD

Toasted walnuts flavour this bread, which should be thinly sliced, toasted, and served with cheese.

450 g (1 lb) LOAF	INGREDIENTS	675 g (1½ lb) LOAF
55 g (1¾ oz)	coarsely chopped walnuts	65 g (2½ oz)
120 ml (4 fl oz)	water	175 ml (6 fl oz)
120 g (4½ oz)	ricotta cheese	175 g (6 oz)
1 tbsp	butter	1½ tbsp
2 tbsp	sugar	3 tbsp
1 tsp	salt	1½ tsp
190 g (7 oz)	bread flour	270 g (10 oz)
130 g (5 oz)	wholewheat flour	195 g (7½ oz)
1½ tsp	yeast	2¼ tsp

METHOD

Spread the walnuts on a small baking sheet and place in a preheated 180°C/350°F/Gas 4 oven for 7 to 12 minutes. Check frequently, stirring and turning. Watch carefully as they can scorch easily. When they are brown, remove and let cool. Finely chop the walnuts by hand or process in a food processor until they are the size of biscuit crumbs.

Put walnuts and remaining ingredients in bread tin in order suggested by your bread machine instructions. Set for wholewheat bread, medium crust. Press Start.

LEFT Kathy's Pepper Cheese Bread

BUTTERMILK CHIVE BREAD

*This bread has a soft texture with a subtle taste of buttermilk
and a more prominent taste of chives.*

450 g (1 lb) LOAF	INGREDIENTS	675 g (1½ lb) LOAF
65 ml (2½ fl oz)	water	125 ml (4 fl oz)
65 ml (2½ fl oz)	buttermilk	125 ml (4 fl oz)
1 tbsp	vegetable oil	1½ tbsp
1 tbsp	sugar	1½ tbsp
3 tbsp	chopped fresh chives	4½ tbsp
1 tsp	salt	1½ tsp
270 g (10 oz)	bread flour	425 g (15 oz)
1½ tsp	yeast	2¼ tsp

METHOD

Put ingredients in bread tin in order suggested by your
bread machine instructions. Set for white bread,
medium crust. Press Start.

GRAIN BREADS

Oatmeal Yoghurt Bread   30

Multi-grain Bread   31

Oatmeal Wholewheat Bread   32

Oatmeal Bread with Ginger
and Toasted Almonds   33

Wholewheat Potato
Sesame Bread   33

Multi-grain Buttermilk
Bread   34

Wild Rice Bread   34

Crunchy Bran Bread   36

Wholewheat Bread
with Egg and Honey   37

Cottage Cheese Graham
Bread   38

Grape-Nut Bread   39

Herbed Wholewheat Bread   40

Low-country Beer Bread
with Brown Rice   40

Cinnamon-Orange Bran
Bread   42

OATMEAL YOGHURT BREAD

This is a sturdy bread with good texture and flavour added by the oatmeal and oat bran. If you wish, you may sprinkle a tablespoon of oatmeal over the top of the dough as it begins its second rising, but do it quickly so the bread machine is not open for long – too much loss of heat will interfere with the rising.

450 g (1 lb) LOAF	INGREDIENTS	675 g (1½ lb) LOAF
40 g (1½ oz)	rolled oats	60 g (2½ oz)
65 ml (2½ fl oz)	very hot water	125 ml (4 fl oz)
175 ml (6 fl oz)	plain yoghurt	275 ml (9 fl oz)
1 tbsp	butter	1½ tbsp
2 tbsp	sugar	3 tbsp
1 tsp	salt	1½ tsp
½ tsp	baking soda	¾ tsp
4 tbsp	oat bran	6 tbsp
220 g (7¾ oz)	bread flour	365 g (12½ oz)
1½ tsp	yeast	2¼ tsp

METHOD

Put the oats in the bread tin. Add the hot water and stir. Let sit 15 minutes. Put remaining ingredients in bread tin in order suggested by your bread machine instructions. Set for white bread, medium crust. Press Start.

MULTI-GRAIN BREAD

This is a substantial bread, with the multi-grain cereal adding crunch to the chewy texture. It is dense, but the egg and wheat gluten help leaven it.

450 g (1 lb) LOAF	INGREDIENTS	675 g (1½ lb) LOAF
65 ml (2½ fl oz)	water	125 ml (4 fl oz)
65 ml (2½ fl oz)	milk	65 ml (2½ fl oz)
1	egg	2
1 tbsp	butter	1½ tbsp
2 tbsp	sugar	3 tbsp
1 tsp	salt	1½ tsp
220 g (7¾ oz)	wholewheat flour	365 g (12½ oz)
30 g (1 oz)	multi-grain cereal	70 g (2½ oz)
2 tbsp	vital wheat gluten	3 tbsp
2 tsp	yeast	1 tbsp

METHOD

Put ingredients in bread tin in order suggested by your bread machine instructions. Set for wholewheat bread, medium crust. Press Start.

The dough should be softer and wetter than usual during kneading because the cereal will absorb liquid during baking. If the bread sinks in the centre during baking, it probably means the cereal did not absorb as much liquid as the seven-grain cereal used in testing this recipe. Next time reduce the amount of water by 1 tablespoon for the 450 g (1 lb) loaf, and by 1½ tablespoons for the 675 g (1½ lb) loaf.

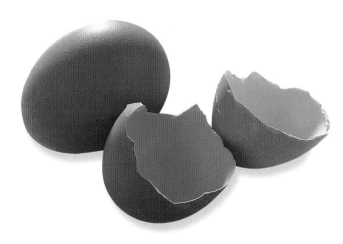

OATMEAL WHOLEWHEAT BREAD

This is a medium-light bread with a good wheat and oat flavour.

450 g (1 lb) LOAF	INGREDIENTS	675 g (1½ lb) LOAF
4 tbsp	water	6 tbsp
125 ml (4 fl oz)	milk	175 ml (6 fl oz)
2 tbsp	vegetable oil	3 tbsp
2 tbsp	honey	3 tbsp
1 tsp	salt	1½ tsp
25 g (1 oz)	rolled oats	40 g (1½ oz)
3 tbsp	toasted wheat germ	4½ tbsp
95 g (3½ oz)	wholewheat flour	190 g (7 oz)
130 g (5 oz)	bread flour	200 g (7½ oz)
2 tsp	yeast	1 tbsp

METHOD

Put ingredients in bread tin in order suggested by your bread machine instructions. Set for wholewheat bread, medium crust. Press Start.

OATMEAL BREAD WITH GINGER AND TOASTED ALMONDS

Toasted almonds and candied ginger give this bread an exotic flavour. It is delicious for toast or in delicately flavoured sandwiches such as cucumber or cream cheese.

450 g (1 lb) LOAF	INGREDIENTS	675 g (1½ lb) LOAF
25 g (1 oz)	slivered almonds	40 g (1½ oz)
25 g (1 oz)	rolled oats	40 g (1½ oz)
85 ml (3 fl oz)	boiling water	120 ml (4 fl oz)
120 ml (4 fl oz)	milk	175 ml (6 fl oz)
2 tbsp	butter	3 tbsp
2 tbsp	sugar	3 tbsp
1 tsp	salt	1½ tsp
2 tbsp	wheat germ	3 tbsp
220 g (7¾ oz)	bread flour	365 g (12½ oz)
1½ tsp	yeast	2¼ tsp
2 tbsp	chopped candied ginger	3 tbsp

METHOD

Spread the almonds on a small baking sheet and toast in a preheated 180°C/350°F/Gas 4 oven for 7 to 12 minutes. Watch closely and stir often until almonds are lightly browned and give off a toasty scent. Let cool. Chop in a food processor until almonds are the size of breadcrumbs.

Put the oats in the bread tin. Pour boiling water over, stir and let set for 15 minutes. When oats have cooled, add ground almonds and remaining ingredients except ginger in order suggested by your bread machine instructions. Set for white bread, medium crust. Press Start. After about 15 minutes or when the beeper signals time to add fruit, add ginger.

Candied ginger can be found in the spice rack or Asian food section of well-stocked supermarkets.

WHOLEWHEAT POTATO SESAME BREAD

This is a hearty bread, lightened with mashed potatoes and potato flour. The toasted sesame seeds, added near the end of the kneading, give the bread its crunch and distinctive nutty flavour.

450 g (1 lb) LOAF	INGREDIENTS	675 g (1½ lb) LOAF
2 tsp	sesame seeds	1 tbsp
90 g (3¼ oz)	mashed potatoes	150 g (5 oz)
175 ml (6 fl oz)	buttermilk	250 ml (8 fl oz)
1 tbsp	butter	1½ tbsp
1 tbsp	sugar	1½ tbsp
1 tsp	salt	1½ tsp
1 tbsp	potato flour	1½ tbsp
135 g (5 oz)	wholewheat flour	200 g (7½ oz)
190 g (7 oz)	bread flour	270 g (10 oz)
1½ tsp	yeast	2¼ tsp

METHOD

Toast the sesame seeds first, so they have time to cool before adding them to the dough. Put the seeds in a small frying pan over medium heat. Watch closely, stirring frequently. As they start to toast, the oil will rise to the surface and they will clump, then begin browning. At this point, reduce heat to low, stir almost constantly and pay close attention because they can scorch quickly. When they are golden brown, remove from heat and let cool.

Put all ingredients except sesame seeds in bread tin in order suggested by your bread machine instructions. Set for wholewheat bread, medium crust. Press Start. After about 15 minutes or when the beeper signals time to add fruit, add sesame seeds.

NOTE

This recipe is based on pure mashed potatoes with no additions. If milk or other liquids have been added to the potatoes, check during kneading and add a little flour if dough is too wet.

MULTI-GRAIN BUTTERMILK BREAD

This is a sturdy wheat bread with lots of texture and bits of flavour from the various grains in the cereal. It is good in sandwiches or for toast.

450 g (1 lb) LOAF	INGREDIENTS	675 g (1½ lb) LOAF
6 tbsp	water	265 ml (8½ fl oz)
125 ml (4 fl oz)	buttermilk	175 ml (6 fl oz)
2 tbsp	vegetable oil	3 tbsp
2 tbsp	honey	3 tbsp
½ tsp	baking soda	¾ tsp
1 tsp	salt	1½ tsp
2 tbsp	vital wheat gluten	3 tbsp
30 g (1 oz)	multi-grain cereal	70 g (2½ oz)
130 g (5 oz)	wholewheat flour	200 g (7½ oz)
95 g (3½ oz)	bread flour	190 g (7 oz)
2 tsp	yeast	1 tbsp

METHOD

Put ingredients in bread tin in order suggested by your bread machine instructions. Set for wholewheat bread, medium crust. Press Start.

WILD RICE BREAD

Flavoured by lemon zest, fresh chives and almonds, this bread has lots of taste and texture.

450 g (1 lb) LOAF	INGREDIENTS	675 g (1½ lb) LOAF
30 g (1 oz)	uncooked wild rice	6 tbsp
120 ml (4 fl oz)	soured cream	175 ml (6 fl oz)
50 ml (2 fl oz)	water	6 tbsp
1 tbsp	butter	1½ tbsp
1 tbsp	sugar	1½ tbsp
1 tsp	grated lemon zest	1½ tsp
2 tbsp	chopped fresh chives	6 tbsp
25 g (¾ oz)	slivered almonds, chopped	6 tbsp
1 tsp	salt	1½ tsp
270 g (10 oz)	bread flour	425 g (15 oz)
1½ tsp	yeast	2¼ tsp

METHOD

To cook wild rice, put it in a pot with lots of salted water and boil for about 1 hour, adding more water if necessary, until all the grains have burst. Wild rice isn't really a rice – it's a grain, so don't expect it to absorb water as rice does. Drain and allow to cool.

Put ingredients in bread tin in order suggested by your bread machine instructions. Set for white bread, medium crust. Press Start.

RIGHT Multi-grain Buttermilk Bread

CRUNCHY BRAN BREAD

This is a chewy, dense bread with a crunch given to it by millet and sunflower seeds. Those of you who like to peep at the dough while it's kneading should not worry if the dough seems too wet. The bran cereal – All-Bran or Fibre One, not bran flakes – will soak it up. The bread is good for toast and sandwiches.

450 g (1 lb) LOAF	INGREDIENTS	675 g (1½ lb) LOAF
150 ml (5 fl oz)	milk	175 ml (6 fl oz)
1	egg	2
2 tbsp	butter	3 tbsp
2 tbsp	honey	3 tbsp
1 tsp	salt	1½ tsp
2 tbsp	millet seed	3 tbsp
30 g (1 oz)	bran cereal	55 g (2 oz)
95 g (3½ oz)	wholewheat flour	190 g (7 oz)
130 g (5 oz)	bread flour	200 g (7½ oz)
2 tsp	yeast	1 tbsp
2 tbsp	raw sunflower seeds	3 tbsp

METHOD

Put all ingredients except sunflower seeds in bread tin in order suggested by your bread machine instructions. Set for wholewheat bread, medium crust. Press Start. After about 15 minutes or when the beeper signals time to add fruit, add sunflower seeds.

WHOLEWHEAT BREAD WITH EGG AND HONEY

This is a solid bread, medium weight, with a faint taste of honey.

450 g (1 lb) LOAF	INGREDIENTS	675 g (1½ lb) LOAF
1	egg	2
125 ml (4 fl oz)	milk	175 ml (6 fl oz)
2 tbsp	vegetable oil	3 tbsp
2 tbsp	honey	3 tbsp
1 tsp	salt	1½ tsp
3 tbsp	toasted wheat germ	4½ tbsp
130 g (5 oz)	wholewheat flour	200 g (7½ oz)
130 g (5 oz)	bread flour	200 g (7½ oz)
1½ tsp	yeast	2¼ tsp

METHOD

Put ingredients in bread tin in order suggested by your bread machine instructions. Set for wholewheat bread, medium crust. Press Start.

Cottage Cheese Graham Bread

This produces a dense, heavy bread with a nubbly texture and good wheat flavour.
Use it for toast and sandwiches.

450 g (1 lb) LOAF	INGREDIENTS	675 g (1½ lb) LOAF
35 g (1½ oz)	bulghur	6 tbsp
500 ml (20 fl oz)	water	425 ml (19 fl oz)
150 g (6 oz)	cottage cheese	210 g (9 oz)
2 tbsp	butter	3 tbsp
1 tbsp	honey	2 tbsp
1 tsp	salt	1½ tsp
130 g (5 oz)	bread flour	200 g (7½ oz)
130 g (5 oz)	graham flour	200 g (7½ oz)
2 tsp	yeast	1 tbsp

METHOD

Put the bulghur in a small pan with 425 ml (19 fl oz) of the water. Bring to the boil and let boil for 6 minutes. Remove from heat and drain. Let cool 15 minutes. Blot with kitchen paper to absorb excess moisture.

Put the cooled bulghur, remaining water and other ingredients in bread tin in order suggested by your bread machine instructions. Set for wholewheat bread, medium crust. Press Start. The stiffness of the dough may vary, depending on the liquid content of the cheese. Watch the dough while it is kneading and add a little flour, 1 tablespoon at a time, if it is too soft. Add water, 1 teaspoon at a time, if the dough is too stiff.

GRAPE-NUT BREAD

*This wholewheat bread is made with one of my favourite breakfast combinations,
Grape Nuts cereal and yoghurt. The cereal gives it a bitey texture, and the yoghurt
gives it a slight tang.*

450 g (1 lb) LOAF	INGREDIENTS	675 g (1½ lb) LOAF
65 ml (2½ fl oz)	water	125 ml (4 fl oz)
175 ml (6 fl oz)	plain yoghurt	250 ml (8 fl oz)
1 tbsp	butter	1½ tbsp
1 tbsp	sugar	1½ tbsp
1 tsp	salt	1½ tsp
30 g (1 oz)	Grape Nuts	70 g (2½ oz)
95 g (3½ oz)	wholewheat flour	130 g (5 oz)
130 g (5 oz)	bread flour	200 g (7½ oz)
1½ tsp	yeast	2¼ tsp

METHOD

Put ingredients in bread tin in order suggested by your
bread machine instructions. Set for wholewheat bread,
medium crust. Press Start.

HERBED WHOLEWHEAT BREAD

A dense bread with substantial heft, this bread is leavened by wheat gluten. It will leave your kitchen fragrant with herbs.

450 g (1 lb) LOAF	INGREDIENTS	675 g (1½ lb) LOAF	METHOD
65 ml (2½ fl oz)	water	125 ml (4 fl oz)	Put ingredients in bread tin in order suggested by your bread machine instructions. Set for wholewheat bread, medium crust. Press Start.
125 ml (4 fl oz)	milk	175 ml (6 fl oz)	
2 tbsp	butter	3 tbsp	
2 tbsp	sugar	3 tbsp	
1 tsp	dried oregano	1½ tsp	
1 tsp	dried basil	1½ tsp	
1 tsp	dried onion flakes	1½ tsp	
1 tsp	salt	1½ tsp	
3 tbsp	wheat germ	4½ tbsp	
2 tbsp	vital wheat gluten	3 tbsp	
270 g (10 oz)	wholewheat flour	425 g (15 oz)	
2 tsp	yeast	1 tbsp	

LOW-COUNTRY BEER BREAD WITH BROWN RICE

From the low country of the Carolinas comes this tasty, chewy bread. Brown rice gives it a hint of nutty sweetness and a substantial texture. For variety and a hint of bitterness, use stout instead of beer.

450 g (1 lb) LOAF	INGREDIENTS	675 g (1½ lb) LOAF	METHOD
1	egg	1 + 1 yolk	Put ingredients in bread tin in order suggested by your bread machine instructions. Set for wholewheat bread, medium crust. Press Start.
120 ml (4 fl oz)	beer	175 ml (6 fl oz)	
1 tbsp	butter	1½ tbsp	
1 tbsp	honey	1½ tbsp	
1 tsp	salt	1½ tsp	
70 g (2½ oz)	cooked brown rice	100 g (4 oz)	
130 g (5 oz)	bread flour	200 g (7½ oz)	
130 g (5 oz)	wholewheat flour	200 g (7½ oz)	
2 tsp	yeast	1 tbsp	

RIGHT Herbed Wholewheat Bread

Cinnamon-Orange Bran Bread

This is a substantial bread with a tender crumb. The bran and sunflower seeds give it texture, while it gets flavour from cinnamon, orange zest and the nuttiness of the sunflower seeds. It makes excellent toast. Use a bran cereal such as All-Bran or Fibre One, not flakes.

450 g (1 lb) LOAF	INGREDIENTS	675 g (1½ lb) LOAF
4 tbsp	water	6 tbsp
125 ml (4 fl oz)	milk	175 ml (6 fl oz)
1 tbsp	butter	1½ tbsp
2 tbsp	honey	3 tbsp
1 tsp	cinnamon	1½ tsp
1 tsp	grated orange zest	1½ tsp
1 tsp	salt	1½ tsp
30 g (1 oz)	bran cereal	55 g (2 oz)
95 g (3½ oz)	wholewheat flour	190 g (7 oz)
130 g (5 oz)	bread flour	200 g (7½ oz)
1½ tsp	yeast	2¼ tsp
2 tbsp	raw sunflower seeds	3 tbsp

METHOD

Put all ingredients except sunflower seeds in bread tin in order suggested by your bread machine instructions. Set for wholewheat bread, medium crust. Press Start. After about 15 minutes or when the beeper signals time to add fruit, add sunflower seeds.

RYE BREADS

Rye Bread   44

Corn Rye Bread   44

Dark Rye Bread   45

Double Rye Bread   46

Raisin Pecan Rye Bread   46

Wholewheat Rye Bread   48

Swedish Rye Bread   49

Dark and Fruity Rye Bread   51

Onion Rye with Semolina   51

Potato Rye with Caraway
and Dill   52

RYE BREAD

This is a very simple rye bread, made with equal parts rye and bread flour.

450 g (1 lb) LOAF	INGREDIENTS	675 g (1½ lb) LOAF
120 ml (4 fl oz)	water	175 ml (6 fl oz)
50 ml (2 fl oz)	milk	6 tbsp
1 tbsp	butter	1½ tbsp
1 tbsp	honey	1½ tbsp
1 tsp	salt	1½ tsp
130 g (5 oz)	rye flour	200 g (7½ oz)
130 g (5 oz)	bread flour	200 g (7½ oz)
2 tsp	yeast	1 tbsp

METHOD

Put ingredients in bread tin in order suggested by your bread machine instructions. Set for wholewheat bread, medium crust. Press Start.

CORN RYE BREAD

Baked in the oven as a round loaf, this makes a dense, flavourful bread that is excellent with cheese or butter or made into small sandwiches.

450 g (1 lb) LOAF	INGREDIENTS	675 g (1½ lb) LOAF
250 ml (8 fl oz)	water	350 ml (12 fl oz)
1 tsp	salt	1½ tsp
2 tbsp	butter	3 tbsp
80 g (2¾ oz)	cornmeal	115 g (4½ oz)
50 ml (2 fl oz)	water	6 tbsp
1 tbsp	sugar	1½ tbsp
1½ tsp	caraway seeds	2¼ tsp
1 tbsp	vital wheat gluten	1½ tbsp
130 g (5 oz)	rye flour	200 g (7½ oz)
130 g (5 oz)	bread flour	200 g (7½ oz)
2 tsp	yeast	1 tbsp

METHOD

Put first quantity of water, salt and butter in a small saucepan and bring to the boil. Add cornmeal in a thin stream, stirring constantly. When mixture forms a paste and boils, reduce heat and allow to boil 1 minute longer. Remove from heat and let cool.

Put cooled cornmeal mixture in bread tin with remaining ingredients in order suggested by your bread machine instructions. Set for wholewheat, dough stage. Press Start.

When dough is ready, punch it down on a lightly floured surface. Shape into a small round. This is a soft dough that will spread out if baked free-form. Using foil that is folded into a long strip, make a collar about 17 to 20 cm (7 to 8 inches) in diameter for the small loaf, 23 to 25 cm (9 to 10 inches) for the larger loaf. Put the dough round on a baking sheet that has been sprinkled with cornmeal and put the foil collar around it. Let rise until doubled in volume, about 1 hour. Bake in a preheated 190°C/375°F/Gas 5 oven until lightly browned, about 30 to 40 minutes.

Dark Rye Bread

This dark pumpernickel bread is full-flavoured with a tender grain. It makes delicious sandwiches and holds up well against strong flavours. Ordinary rye flour can be substituted for the coarser pumpernickel flour, and will produce a smoother texture.

450 g (1 lb) LOAF	INGREDIENTS	675 g (1½ lb) LOAF
6 tbsp	milk	175 ml (6 fl oz)
6 tbsp	strong coffee	125 ml (4 fl oz)
2 tbsp	vegetable oil	3 tbsp
3 tbsp	molasses, preferably dark	50 ml (2 fl oz)
1 tsp	salt	1½ tsp
1 tbsp	unsweetened cocoa	1½ tbsp
1 tbsp	caraway seeds	1½ tbsp
2 tbsp	cornmeal	3 tbsp
185 g (6½ oz)	bread flour	270 g (10 oz)
95 g (3½ oz)	pumpernickel flour	130 g (5 oz)
2 tsp	yeast	1 tbsp

METHOD

Put ingredients in bread tin in order suggested by your bread machine instructions. Set for wholewheat bread, medium crust. Press Start.

DOUBLE RYE BREAD

This rye bread is made with rye berries, which must be cooked in advance, drained and cooled. It makes a very dense, compact loaf with good rye flavour and lots of texture. It is best served warm, thinly sliced with butter.

450 g (1 lb) LOAF	INGREDIENTS	675 g (1½ lb) LOAF
2 tbsp	rye berries	3 tbsp
65 ml (2½ fl oz)	milk	125 ml (4 fl oz)
50 ml (2 fl oz)	water	50 ml (2 fl oz)
1	egg	2
2 tbsp	vegetable oil	3 tbsp
1 tbsp	honey	1½ tbsp
1 tsp	salt	1½ tsp
2 tsp	caraway seeds	1 tbsp
130 g (5 oz)	rye flour	200 g (7½ oz)
130 g (5 oz)	bread flour	200 g (7½ oz)
1 tbsp	vital wheat gluten	1½ tbsp
2 tsp	yeast	1 tbsp

METHOD

Put the rye berries in a saucepan with lots of water. Bring to the boil and let boil for 1 hour, checking occasionally to be sure the water has not boiled away. Bite one of the grains. If it is hard to chew, let boil for another 10 minutes, then check again until grains are tender-chewy. Drain and let cool for at least 30 minutes.

Put cooled rye berries and remaining ingredients in bread tin in order suggested by your bread machine instructions. Set for wholewheat bread, medium crust. Press Start.

RAISIN PECAN RYE BREAD

This is a tasty bread with a sturdy texture. It's good with butter and mild cheese, and for toast.

450 g (1 lb) LOAF	INGREDIENTS	675 g (1½ lb) LOAF
175 ml (6 fl oz)	water	275 ml (9 fl oz)
2 tbsp	vegetable oil	3 tbsp
1 tbsp	sugar	1½ tbsp
1 tsp	salt	1½ tsp
2 tbsp	cornmeal	3 tbsp
180 g (6 oz)	bread flour	295 g (11 oz)
95 g (3½ oz)	rye flour	190 g (7 oz)
2 tsp	yeast	1 tbsp
4 tbsp	raisins	6 tbsp
4 tbsp	chopped pecans	6 tbsp

METHOD

Put all dough ingredients except raisins and nuts in bread tin in order suggested by your bread machine instructions. Set for wholewheat bread, medium crust. Press Start. After about 15 minutes or when the beeper signals time to add fruit, add raisins and pecans.

When dough is ready, punch it down on a lightly floured board. Let it rest a few minutes. Then take it between your hands and roll it into a rope, about 37 cm (15 inches) long for the smaller recipe, 45 to 50 cm (18 to 20 inches) for the larger recipe. Put it on a nonstick or lightly buttered baking sheet. Bring the ends together to form a circle. Cover and let rise for 45 to 60 minutes.

With a sharp knife, make diagonal slashes about 5 cm (2 inches) apart in the top of the bread. Bake in a preheated 180°C/350°F/Gas 4 oven for 35 to 55 minutes, until the top is golden brown.

RIGHT Raisin Pecan Rye Bread

WHOLEWHEAT RYE BREAD

*This is a good basic bread with a mild taste. Made with three kinds of flour and
extra wheat gluten, it is not as light as white bread but nor is it a dense bread.*

450 g (1 lb) LOAF	INGREDIENTS	675 g (1½ lb) LOAF
4 tbsp	water	6 tbsp
125 ml (4 fl oz)	milk	175 ml (6 fl oz)
2 tbsp	butter	3 tbsp
1 tbsp	sugar	1½ tbsp
1 tsp	salt	1½ tsp
95 g (3½ oz)	bread flour	130 g (5 oz)
95 g (3½ oz)	wholewheat flour	130 g (5 oz)
95 g (3½ oz)	rye flour	130 g (5 oz)
1 tbsp	vital wheat gluten	1½ tbsp
2 tsp	yeast	1 tbsp

METHOD

Put ingredients in bread tin in order suggested by your
bread machine instructions. Set for wholewheat bread,
medium crust. Press Start.

SWEDISH RYE BREAD

This is a light rye bread with a lot of flavour – molasses, nutmeg and carrots, dominated by orange. It is good just buttered or for toast, but flavours may clash with some sandwich fillings. Try it with turkey and cranberry sauce.

450 g (1 lb) LOAF	INGREDIENTS	675 g (1½ lb) LOAF
4 tbsp	water	6 tbsp
65 ml (2½ fl oz)	milk	125 ml (4 fl oz)
1 tbsp	vegetable oil	1½ tbsp
2 tbsp	molasses	3 tbsp
¼ tsp	ground nutmeg	½ tsp
1 tsp	grated orange zest	1½ tsp
4 tbsp	grated carrots	6 tbsp
1 tsp	salt	1½ tsp
185 g (6½ oz)	bread flour	270 g (10 oz)
95 g (3½ oz)	rye flour	130 g (5 oz)
1½ tsp	yeast	2¼ tsp

METHOD

Put ingredients in bread tin in order suggested by your bread machine instructions. Set for wholewheat bread, medium crust. Press Start.

DARK AND FRUITY RYE BREAD

*This rye bread is tender and slightly sweet. It is made with ale, lemon zest, raisins
and candied orange peel, and sweetened with molasses.*

450 g (1 lb) LOAF	INGREDIENTS	675 g (1½ lb) LOAF
175 ml (6 fl oz)	dark stout or ale	250 ml (8 fl oz)
2 tbsp	powdered milk	3 tbsp
2 tbsp	vegetable oil	3 tbsp
2 tbsp	molasses	3 tbsp
1 tsp	grated lemon zest	1½ tsp
1 tbsp	unsweetened cocoa	1½ tbsp
1 tsp	salt	1½ tsp
95 g (3½ oz)	rye flour	130 g (5 oz)
185 g (6½ oz)	bread flour	270 g (10 oz)
2 tsp	yeast	1 tbsp
4 tbsp	raisins	6 tbsp
1 tbsp	candied orange peel, minced	1½ tbsp

METHOD

Put all ingredients except raisins and candied orange
peel in bread tin in order suggested by your bread
machine instructions. Set for wholewheat bread,
medium crust. Press Start. After about 15 minutes or
when the beeper signals time to add fruit, add raisins
and orange peel.

ONION RYE WITH SEMOLINA

This makes a crusty onion-flavoured baguette.

450 g (1 lb) LOAF	INGREDIENTS	675 g (1½ lb) LOAF
165 ml (5½ fl oz)	water	250 ml (8 fl oz)
1 tbsp	sugar	1½ tbsp
1 tbsp	olive oil	1½ tbsp
2 tsp	dried onion flakes	1 tbsp
1 tsp	salt	1½ tsp
95 g (3½ oz)	bread flour	130 g (5 oz)
95 g (3½ oz)	rye flour	130 g (5 oz)
95 g (3½ oz)	semolina flour	130 g (5 oz)
1 tbsp	vital wheat gluten	1½ tbsp
2 tsp	yeast	1 tbsp

METHOD

Put ingredients in bread tin in order suggested by your
bread machine instructions. Set for wholewheat bread,
dough stage. Press Start.

When dough is ready, punch it down on a lightly
floured board. Let it rest a few minutes. Then take it
between your hands and roll it into a fat log, 25 to 30
cm (10 to 12 inches) long for the smaller loaf, 40 to 45
cm (15 to 18 inches) for the larger loaf. Put the bread
on a baking sheet that has been sprinkled with
cornmeal or in a buttered baguette tin. Cover and let
rise for 45 to 60 minutes. Bake in a preheated
190°C/375°F/Gas 5 oven for about 30 to 45 minutes.

LEFT Dark and Fruity Rye Bread

POTATO RYE WITH CARAWAY AND DILL

This is a dense, hearty bread, fragrant with dill and caraway. It can be made without the vital wheat gluten, but will not rise a lot. This bread is excellent for meat sandwiches.

450 g (1 lb) LOAF	INGREDIENTS	675 g (1½ lb) LOAF
90 g (3¼ oz)	mashed potatoes	150 g (5 oz)
125 ml (4 fl oz)	water	175 ml (6 fl oz)
1 tbsp	vegetable oil	1½ tbsp
1 tbsp	sugar	1½ tbsp
1½ tsp	caraway seeds	2¼ tsp
1 tsp	dried dill	1½ tsp
1 tsp	salt	1½ tsp
130 g (5 oz)	bread flour	200 g (7½ oz)
130 g (5 oz)	rye flour	200 g (7½ oz)
1 tbsp	vital wheat gluten	1½ tbsp
2 tsp	yeast	1 tbsp

METHOD

Put ingredients in bread tin in order suggested by your bread machine instructions. Set for wholewheat bread, medium crust. Press Start.

NOTE

This recipe is based on pure mashed potatoes with no additions. If milk or other liquids have been added to the potatoes, check during kneading and add a little flour if dough is too wet.

SOURDOUGH BREADS

Sourdough Starter   54

Sourdough Bread   55

Sourdough Rye Raisin Bread   56

Sourdough Bread with
Roasted Garlic and Peppers   57

Sourdough Rosemary Bread
with Olives   58

Wholewheat
Sourdough Bread
with Sun-dried Tomatoes   60

Wholewheat Sourdough
with Bulghur   61

Southwestern Spiced
Sourdough   63

Sisteron Rye Bread   64

Sourdough Rye Seed Bread   65

SOURDOUGH STARTER

Sourdough is often associated with the crusty, dense loaves for which San Francisco is famous, but its use in baking can be traced back to ancient Egypt, when much effort was made to disguise the sour taste. Sourdough is the product of fermentation in dough that has sat open to the air in warm temperatures for several days, gathering wild yeasts from the air.
Theoretically, a bread made with a good sourdough starter will not need any additional yeast as leavening, but such breads are often too dense and unleavened to suit most people's tastes. Today, sourdough starter is added to bread not for leavening, but to give it that sour taste that bakers once tried to disguise. Making and maintaining your own pot of sourdough starter is not difficult, especially if you bake frequently. The first batch takes several days to develop a good sour taste, but after that it can be used and replenished daily.

INGREDIENTS

250 ml (8 fl oz) low-fat milk, scalded
250 ml (8 fl oz) hot water
1 tbsp sugar
2¼ tsp active dry yeast
350 g (12 oz) plain or bread flour

METHOD

Mix the milk, hot water and sugar. Let cool to between 40°C (105°F) and 45°C (115°F), then add the yeast. Let sit until the mixture develops a foamy head, about 5 to 10 minutes. Then add the flour and mix well.

Loosely cover the bowl with a lid that is partly ajar and put it in a warm place, between 27°C (80°F) and 38°C (100°F). Leaving the bowl partly uncovered allows air to circulate and airborne yeasts to collect in the starter. Within 24 hours, it should be bubbly and develop a hint of a sour smell. Stir it once or twice a day. The mixture may separate, with a thick, gluey mixture at the bottom and a watery liquid floating on top. That's normal; just stir together. The starter is ready when it develops a good sour smell, usually three to five days.

To bake sourdough bread, you need to prepare a "sponge" at least six hours in advance. Mix some starter with a portion of flour and liquid, as directed by the recipe. Replenish the starter with amounts of flour and water equal to the amount you removed. For instance, if the recipe calls for 125 ml (4 fl oz) of sourdough starter, replenish the starter with 125 ml (4 fl oz) water and 115 g (4 oz) flour. Both the sponge and the replenished starter should be put in a warm place, covered loosely, and left to ferment at least 6 hours, until bubbly.

If you use the starter frequently, more or less daily, you can leave it in its warm place all the time, replenishing it after each use. If you use it only occasionally, replenish it, let it stand 24 hours, then cover tightly and refrigerate. If you don't bake at least weekly, refresh the starter every week or so. Remove 250 ml (8 fl oz) of the starter and discard the rest. Add 130 g (5 oz) of flour and 250 ml (8 fl oz) water, let it stand for 24 hours, then refrigerate.

NOTES

Every six months or so, add a pinch of sugar and yeast to the starter.

The starter will never look attractive; grey is its normal colour. However, if the starter or the liquid develops a green or a pink cast, throw the whole thing out and start again.

SOURDOUGH BREAD

*Sourdough can be stubborn and temperamental, and the bread it makes can vary
with each baking. Because the starter is left open to collect wild yeasts from the air,
one sourdough loaf can taste different from the next. In addition, the dough may
require varying amounts of liquid because the starter also absorbs varying amounts
of liquid from the air. Be patient, watch the dough as the bread machine kneads it
and add a splash of water or a tablespoon of flour as necessary.
A traditional French sourdough loaf is made without sugar or fat. We have included
a small amount of each – sugar to encourage the yeast to ferment, and butter so that
the bread does not turn stale and hard too quickly. Purists can omit both.*

450 g (1 lb) LOAF	INGREDIENTS	675 g (1½ lb) LOAF
	SOURDOUGH SPONGE	
65 ml (2½ fl oz)	sourdough starter	120 ml (4 fl oz)
4 tbsp	water	6 tbsp
95 g (3½ oz)	bread flour	150 g (5 oz)
	BREAD	
5 tbsp	water	7½ tbsp
2 tsp	sugar	1 tbsp
1 tbsp	butter	1½ tbsp
185 g (6½ oz)	bread flour	270 g (10 oz)
1 tsp	salt	1½ tsp
1½ tsp	yeast	2¼ tsp

EGG WASH (OPTIONAL)

1 egg, beaten with a fork

2 tsp water

METHOD

At least 12 hours before baking, make the sourdough
sponge by combining the sourdough starter, water and
flour. Stir and leave in a warm place overnight.

When you are ready to bake, put the sourdough sponge
and all the bread ingredients in bread tin in order
suggested by your bread machine instructions. Set for
dough. Press Start. You may need to adjust liquid or
flour slightly, depending on the water content of your
sourdough starter.

When dough is ready, punch it down on a lightly
floured board. Let it rest a few minutes. Sprinkle
cornmeal on a baking sheet. Shape the dough into a
round and put it on the baking sheet. Cover and let rise
in a warm place for 1 hour.

Combine the egg and water, if using, and brush over the
top of the dough. With a sharp knife, make three
slashes in the top of the bread. Place in a preheated
190°C/375°F/Gas 5 oven and bake until the top is
golden brown, 30 to 50 minutes.

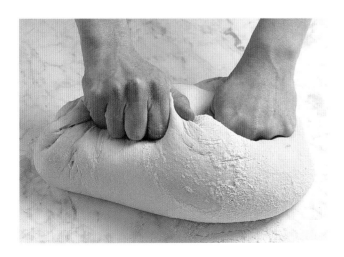

SOURDOUGH RYE RAISIN BREAD

This is a chewy sourdough with good flavour and a hint of sweetness added by the molasses and raisins.

450 g (1 lb) LOAF	INGREDIENTS	675 g (1½ lb) LOAF
	SOURDOUGH SPONGE	
65 ml (2½ fl oz)	sourdough starter	125 ml (4 fl oz)
4 tbsp	water	6 tbsp
95 g (3½ oz)	rye flour	130 g (5 oz)
	BREAD	
4 tbsp	water	6 tbsp
1 tbsp	butter	1½ tbsp
2 tbsp	molasses	3 tbsp
1 tbsp	unsweetened cocoa	1½ tbsp
1 tsp	salt	1½ tsp
185 g (6½ oz)	bread flour	270 g (10 oz)
1½ tsp	yeast	2¼ tsp
40 g (1½ oz)	raisins	50 g (2 oz)

EGG WASH

1 egg, beaten with a fork

2 tsp water

METHOD

At least 12 hours before baking, make the sourdough sponge by combining the sourdough starter, water and rye flour. Stir and leave in a warm place overnight.

Put sourdough sponge in bread tin along with all the bread ingredients except the raisins in the order suggested by your bread machine instructions. Set for dough. Press Start. You may need to adjust liquid or flour slightly, depending on the water content of your sourdough starter.

When dough is ready, punch it down on a lightly floured board. Let it rest a few minutes. Sprinkle cornmeal on a baking sheet. Shape the dough into a round and put it on the baking sheet. Cover, put in a warm place and let rise until doubled in bulk, 45 to 60 minutes. Combine the egg and water and brush over the top of the dough. With a sharp knife, make three slashes in the top of the bread. Place in a preheated 190°C/375°F/Gas 5 oven and bake until the top is golden brown, about 30 to 45 minutes.

SOURDOUGH BREAD WITH ROASTED GARLIC AND PEPPERS

Roasted sweet red peppers are the dominant flavour here, backed up by thyme and a subtle taste of garlic.

450 g (1 lb) LOAF	INGREDIENTS	675 g (1½ lb) LOAF
	SOURDOUGH SPONGE	
65 ml (2½ fl oz)	sourdough starter	125 ml (4 fl oz)
4 tbsp	water	6 tbsp
95 g (3½ oz)	bread flour	130 g (5 oz)
	BREAD	
1 small	whole garlic bulb	1 large
1 tbsp	olive oil	1 tbsp
½ medium	roasted red pepper, chopped	1 large
3 tbsp	water	4½ tbsp
2 tsp	sugar	1 tbsp
1 tsp	salt	1½ tsp
185 g (6½ oz)	bread flour	270 g (10 oz)
1½ tsp	yeast	2¼ tsp

METHOD

At least 12 hours before baking, make the sourdough sponge by combining the sourdough starter, water and flour. Stir and leave in a warm place overnight.

To roast the garlic, remove the outer papery husks. Put on a doubled piece of kitchen foil, pour olive oil over top of garlic and turn so all surfaces are oiled. Wrap the foil around the garlic so it is completely enclosed. Bake in a 180°C/350°F/Gas 4 oven for about 40 minutes, until cloves are soft like butter. Remove from oven and let cool, then cut open each clove and squeeze out the garlic.

To roast red pepper, cut about half a pepper into several fairly flat pieces. Put on a grill pan or a flat piece of kitchen foil, skin side up. Place under the grill and cook until skin is blackened and blistered. Remove and put immediately in a paper bag or a covered dish so pepper can steam as it cools. This loosens the skin. When pepper is cool enough to handle, peel off and discard skin – it's OK if a few bits remain – and dice pepper.

Put sourdough sponge, garlic and remaining ingredients except peppers in bread tin in order suggested by your bread machine instructions. Set for white bread, dough stage. Press Start. After about 15 minutes or when the beeper signals time to add fruit, add diced pepper.

When dough is ready, punch it down on a lightly floured board. Let it rest a few minutes. Sprinkle cornmeal on a baking sheet. Shape the dough into a round and put it on the baking sheet. Cover and let rise in a warm place for 1 hour.

With a sharp knife, make three slashes in the top of the bread, then make three more slashes at a diagonal. Place in a preheated 190°C/375°F/Gas 5 oven and bake until the top is golden brown, 35 to 45 minutes.

SOURDOUGH ROSEMARY BREAD WITH OLIVES

*This is a tantalizing sourdough bread, fragrant with rosemary and studded with
bits of olive. It is best served warm with sweet butter but is also delicious with
strong cheeses.*

450 g (1 lb) LOAF	INGREDIENTS	675 g (1½ lb) LOAF
	SOURDOUGH SPONGE	
65 ml (2½ fl oz)	sourdough starter	125 ml (4 fl oz)
4 tbsp	water	6 tbsp
95 g (3½ oz)	bread flour	130 g (5 oz)
	BREAD	
1 tsp	chopped fresh rosemary	1½ tsp
2 tbsp	olive oil	3 tbsp
5 tbsp	water	7½ tbsp
185 g (6½ oz)	bread flour	270 g (10 oz)
1 tsp	salt	1½ tsp
1½ tsp	yeast	2¼ tsp
4 tbsp	coarsely chopped kalamata olives	6 tbsp

EGGWASH

1 egg, beaten with a fork
2 tsp water

METHOD

At least 12 hours before baking, make the sourdough sponge by combining the sourdough starter, water and flour. Stir and leave in a warm place overnight.

When you are ready to bake, put the rosemary in a small microwave-safe dish with the olive oil. Heat until the oil is hot and the rosemary barely starts to sizzle in the microwave, about 90 seconds on High. Let the rosemary steep in the oil at least 15 minutes, then strain and discard the rosemary. Save the oil for the bread. (You can also heat the oil on the cooker top in a small pan, add the rosemary and remove from the heat.)

Put the sourdough sponge, the rosemary oil and all the bread ingredients except the olives in bread tin in order suggested by your bread machine instructions. Set for dough. Press Start. You may need to adjust liquid or flour slightly, depending on the water content of your sourdough starter. After about 15 minutes or when the beeper signals time to add fruit, add olives.

When dough is ready, punch it down on a lightly floured board. Let it rest a few minutes. Sprinkle cornmeal on a baking sheet. Shape the dough into a round and put it on the baking sheet. Cover and let rise in a warm place for 1 hour.

Combine the egg and water and brush over the top of the dough. With a sharp knife, make three slashes in the top of the bread. Place in a preheated 190°C/375°F/Gas 5 oven and bake until the top is golden brown, 30 to 50 minutes.

WHOLEWHEAT SOURDOUGH BREAD WITH SUN-DRIED TOMATOES

This crusty round of bread, flavoured with sun-dried tomatoes, thyme and crushed pepper, is delicious topped with cheese or in a meatloaf sandwich.

450 g (1 lb) LOAF	INGREDIENTS	675 g (1½ lb) LOAF
	SOURDOUGH SPONGE	
65 ml (2½ fl oz)	sourdough starter	125 ml (4 fl oz)
4 tbsp	water	6 tbsp
95 g (3½ oz)	wholewheat flour	130 g (5 oz)
	BREAD	
3 tbsp	water	4½ tbsp
1 tbsp	olive oil	1½ tbsp
1 tbsp	sugar	1½ tbsp
1 tsp	dried thyme	1½ tsp
1½ tsp	crushed black pepper	2¼ tsp
1 tsp	salt	1½ tsp
185 g (6½ oz)	bread flour	270 g (10 oz)
2 tsp	yeast	1 tbsp
4 tbsp	chopped sun-dried tomatoes	6 tbsp

METHOD

At least 12 hours before baking, make the sourdough sponge by combining the sourdough starter, water and whole-wheat flour. Stir and leave in a warm place overnight.

If tomatoes are stored in oil, blot dry. You can substitute the tomato oil for the olive oil, if you wish.

Put sourdough sponge and all other ingredients except tomatoes in bread tin in order suggested by your bread machine instructions. Set for wholewheat bread, dough stage. Press Start. After about 15 minutes or when the beeper signals time to add fruit, add tomatoes.

When dough is ready, punch it down on a lightly floured board. Let it rest for a few minutes. Sprinkle cornmeal on a baking sheet. Shape the dough into a round and put it on the baking sheet. Cover and let rise in a warm place for 1 hour.

With a sharp knife, make three slashes in the top of the bread, then make three more slashes at a diagonal. Place in a preheated 190°C/375°F/Gas 5 oven and bake until the top is golden brown, 30 to 45 minutes.

WHOLEWHEAT SOURDOUGH WITH BULGHUR

This sourdough bread, baked in the bread machine, gets its slightly coarse texture from the bulghur wheat. Perhaps more than other sourdough breads, the liquid content varies depending on the sourdough starter and how well the bulghur is drained, so the dough should be monitored during the kneading stage and liquid adjusted if needed.

450 g (1 lb) LOAF	INGREDIENTS	675 g (1½ lb) LOAF
	SOURDOUGH SPONGE	
65 ml (2½ fl oz)	sourdough starter	125 ml (4 fl oz)
4 tbsp	water	6 tbsp
95 g (3½ oz)	wholewheat flour	130 g (5 oz)
	BREAD	
4 tbsp	bulghur	6 tbsp
450 ml (16 fl oz)	water	450 ml (16 fl oz)
about 4 tbsp	milk	about 6 tbsp
1 tbsp	butter	1½ tbsp
1 tbsp	sugar	1½ tbsp
1 tsp	salt	1½ tsp
185 g (6½ oz)	bread flour	270 g (10 oz)
2 tsp	yeast	1 tbsp

METHOD

At least 12 hours before baking, make the sourdough sponge by combining the sourdough starter, water and wholewheat flour. Stir and leave in a warm place overnight.

Just before starting the bread, put the bulghur wheat in a small pan with the water. Bring to the boil and let boil for 6 minutes. Remove from heat and drain. Let cool 15 minutes. Blot with kitchen paper to absorb any excess moisture.

Put sourdough sponge, bulgur and remaining ingredients in bread tin in order suggested by your bread machine instructions. Set for wholewheat bread, medium crust. Press Start. Check consistency of dough during kneading and add milk or a little flour if needed.

SOUTHWESTERN SPICED SOURDOUGH

This bread, which is also good when baked in the oven as a free-form loaf, is spiced with the traditional seasonings of the US Southwest – pure chilli powder, ground cumin and oregano, preferably Mexican oregano. Use chilli powder to suit your taste. I like it made with ancho chilli powder, which is only moderately spicy. Take care if using hot New Mexico chilli powder or cayenne. The spice labelled simply "chilli powder" is not pure chilli powder but a blend of chilli and other spices. The bread is studded with pumpkin seeds, which are eaten like sunflower seeds. Called pepitas *in Spanish, shelled pumpkin seeds can be found in Mexican food stores and well-stocked delicatessens. If you use pumpkin seeds that are salted and roasted, reduce the salt in the recipe by ¼ teaspoon.*

450 g (1 lb) LOAF	INGREDIENTS	675 g (1½ lb) LOAF
	SOURDOUGH SPONGE	
65 ml (2½ fl oz)	sourdough starter	120 ml (4 fl oz)
50 ml (2 fl oz)	water	6 tbsp
80 g (3½ oz)	bread flour	150 g (5 oz)
	BREAD	
3 tbsp	water	4½ tbsp
1 tbsp	butter	1½ tbsp
1 tbsp	sugar	1½ tbsp
1 tsp	salt	1½ tsp
1 tbsp	pure chilli powder	1½ tbsp
½ tsp	ground cumin	¾ tsp
1 tsp	dried oregano	1½ tsp
185 g (6½ oz)	bread flour	270 g (10 oz)
1½ tsp	yeast	2¼ tsp
3 tbsp	shelled pumpkin seeds	4½ tbsp

TOPPING
(if baked in the oven)

1 egg
2 tsp water
shelled pumpkin seeds

METHOD

At least 12 hours before baking, make the sourdough sponge by combining the sourdough starter, water and flour. Stir and leave in a warm place overnight.

Put sponge and all bread ingredients except pumpkin seeds in bread tin in order suggested by your bread machine instructions. Set for white bread, medium crust. Press Start. After about 15 minutes or when the beeper signals time to add fruit, add the pumpkin seeds.

To bake this bread in the oven, set the bread machine for dough stage. When it is ready, remove and punch down dough. Shape dough into a round and put on a baking sheet sprinkled with cornmeal.

Combine the egg and water and brush over the bread. Sprinkle some pumpkin seeds over the top.

Cover and let rise in a warm place until doubled in size, about 1 hour. With a sharp knife, make two parallel slashes in the top of the loaf. Bake in a preheated 190°C/375°F/Gas 5 oven until brown, about 30 to 45 minutes.

SISTERON RYE BREAD

This is a sourdough adaptation of the round loaves of rye bread baked in the town of Sisteron, Provence. It is a dense bread, wonderful warm with sweet butter.

SOURDOUGH SPONGE

65 ml (2½ fl oz)	sourdough starter	120 ml (4 fl oz)
50 ml (2 fl oz)	water	6 tbsp
80 g (3½ oz)	pumpernickel flour	150 g (5 oz)
2 tsp	caraway seeds	1 tbsp

BREAD

65 ml (2½ fl oz)	water	120 ml (4 fl oz)
1 tsp	salt	1½ tsp
185 g (6½ oz)	bread flour	270 g (10 oz)
2 tsp	yeast	1 tbsp

TOPPING

1 egg
2 tsp water
caraway seeds, optional

METHOD

At least 12 hours before baking, make the sourdough sponge by combining the sourdough starter, water, pumpernickel flour, and caraway seeds. Stir and leave in a warm place overnight.

Put sourdough sponge and all the bread ingredients in bread tin in order suggested by your bread machine instructions. Set for dough. Press Start.

When dough is ready, punch it down on a lightly floured board. Let it rest a few minutes. Sprinkle cornmeal on a baking sheet. Shape the dough into a round and put it on the baking sheet. Cover and let rise in a warm place for 1 hour.

When dough has risen, combine the egg and water and brush over the top of the dough. With a sharp knife, cut a ring around the top of the dough. Sprinkle caraway seeds over top, if desired. Bake in a preheated 190°C/375°F/Gas 5 oven until golden brown, 30 to 45 minutes.

SOURDOUGH RYE SEED BREAD

This crusty loaf is covered with a mix of five seeds – poppy, sesame, fennel, caraway and flax – that give it unusual crunch and flavour, and a bakery-fresh appearance.

450 g (1 lb) LOAF	INGREDIENTS	675 g (1½ lb) LOAF
SOURDOUGH SPONGE		
65 ml (2½ fl oz)	sourdough starter	125 ml (4 fl oz)
4 tbsp	water	6 tbsp
95 g (3½ oz)	rye flour	130 g (5 oz)
BREAD		
3 tbsp	water	4½ tbsp
1 tbsp	sugar	1½ tbsp
1 tsp	salt	1½ tsp
185 g (6½ oz)	bread flour	270 g (10 oz)
1½ tsp	yeast	2¼ tsp

TOPPINGS

1 egg, lightly beaten with 2 tsp water
For the 450-g (1-pound) loaf; 2 teaspoons each fennel,
caraway, poppy, sesame and flax seeds
For the 675-g (1½-pound) loaf: 1 tablespoon each fennel,
caraway, poppy, sesame and flax seeds

METHOD

At least 12 hours before baking, make the sourdough sponge by combining the sourdough starter, water and flour. Stir and leave in a warm place overnight.

Put sourdough sponge and all the bread ingredients in bread tin in order suggested by your bread machine instructions. Set for wholewheat bread, dough stage. Press Start.

When dough is ready, punch it down on a lightly floured board. Let it rest a few minutes. Then take it between your hands and roll it into a fat log, 25 to 30 cm (10 to 12 inches) long for the smaller loaf, 40 to 45 cm (15 to 18 inches) for the larger loaf. Brush with the egg wash.

Mix the seeds and spread them on a clean surface. Roll the top and sides of the bread in the seeds until loaf is thickly covered and all the seeds have been picked up. Put the bread on a baking sheet that has been sprinkled with cornmeal.

Cover and let rise 45 to 60 minutes. Bake in a preheated 190°C/375°F/Gas 5 oven until top is golden and sounds hollow when tapped, about 30 to 45 minutes.

Pumpkin Graham Bread   67

Potato Bread
with Roasted Garlic   68

Carrot Ginger Wholewheat
Bread   70

Sweet Potato Wholewheat
Bread   71

Jalapeño Cheese Bread   72

Onion Cheese Bread   73

Apple Sauce Oat Bran Bread   75

Cuban Bread with Yuca   75

Oatmeal Raisin Bread   76

Pineapple Orange Bran Bread   77

Coconut Date Bread   77

Pear Wholewheat Bread   78

Sweet Potato Apple Pecan
Bread   80

Date-Nut Wheat Bread   81

Apricot Pecan Anadama Bread   82

Semolina Bread with
Courgette and Millet   83

Apple-Cranberry Graham
Bread   84

FRUIT AND VEGETABLE BREADS

PUMPKIN GRAHAM BREAD

Don't be put off by the orange hues of this tasty bread. It has a slightly chewy texture, a subtle pumpkin flavour and a spicy aroma. It is not a sweet bread, but is delicious for toast with jam and makes a good turkey sandwich.

450 g (1 lb) LOAF	INGREDIENTS	675 g (1½ lb) LOAF
65 ml (2½ fl oz)	milk	125 ml (4 fl oz)
175 ml (6 fl oz)	puréed pumpkin	275 ml (9 fl oz)
2 tbsp	butter	3 tbsp
2 tbsp	sugar	3 tbsp
1 tsp	cinnamon	1½ tsp
½ tsp	ground nutmeg	¾ tsp
1 tsp	salt	1½ tsp
130 g (5 oz)	bread flour	200 g (7½ oz)
130 g (5 oz)	graham flour	200 g (7½ oz)
1½ tsp	yeast	2¼ tsp

METHOD

Put ingredients in bread tin in order suggested by your bread machine instructions. Set for wholewheat bread, medium crust. Press Start.

The stiffness of the dough may vary, depending on the liquid content of the pumpkin. Watch the dough while it is kneading and add a little flour, 1 tablespoon at a time, if it is too soft. Add water, 1 teaspoon at a time, if the dough is too stiff.

POTATO BREAD WITH ROASTED GARLIC

Although this bread will fill your kitchen with heady fragrances of cheese and garlic, the flavour of the bread is subtle. It is best served warm with butter.

450 g (1 lb) LOAF	INGREDIENTS	675 g (1½ lb) LOAF
6–8	garlic cloves	10–12
1 tbsp	olive oil	1 tbsp
2 tbsp	milk	3 tbsp
60 ml (4 fl oz)	water	6 tbsp
115 g (4 oz)	mashed potatoes	175 g (6 oz)
2 tbsp	butter	3 tbsp
1 tbsp	sugar	1½ tbsp
25 g (1 oz)	grated Parmesan cheese	40 g (1½ oz)
½ tsp	fresh-ground black pepper	¾ tsp
1 tsp	salt	1½ tsp
270 g (10 oz)	bread flour	425 g (15 oz)
2 tsp	yeast	1 tbsp

METHOD

Preheat oven to 180°C/350°F/Gas 4. Put garlic cloves, unpeeled, in a square of kitchen foil. Brush with the olive oil. Fold the foil around the cloves. Bake for 30 minutes, or until garlic is soft. Let sit until cloves are cool enough to handle. Then cut open the top of each clove and squeeze out the garlic.

Put the garlic and other ingredients in bread tin in order suggested by your bread machine instructions. Set for white bread, medium crust. Press Start.

NOTE

This recipe is based on pure mashed potatoes with no additions. If milk or other liquids have been added to the potatoes, check during kneading and add a little flour if dough is too wet.

TIP

If you use freshly grated cheese, pack it tightly or much of the measurement will be air.

CARROT GINGER WHOLEWHEAT BREAD

This is a bread with a light texture, mildly flavoured by carrots and ginger. Despite the exotic sound, it is a fine sandwich bread that won't clash with most ingredients.

450 g (1 lb) LOAF	INGREDIENTS	675 g (1½ lb) LOAF
4 tbsp	water	6 tbsp
4 tbsp	milk	6 tbsp
80 g (3 oz)	grated carrots	100 g (4 oz)
2 tbsp	vegetable oil	3 tbsp
2 tbsp	honey	3 tbsp
1 tsp	salt	1½ tsp
1½ tsp	ground ginger	2¼ tsp
3 tbsp	wheat germ	4½ tbsp
180 g (6 oz)	bread flour	295 g (11 oz)
130 g (5 oz)	wholewheat flour	190 g (7 oz)
1½ tsp	yeast	2¼ tsp

METHOD

Put ingredients in bread tin in order suggested by your bread machine instructions. Set for wholewheat bread, medium crust. Press Start.

Sweet Potato Wholewheat Bread

The flavour of sweet potatoes is very subtle in this bread, and it is not a sweet bread. The bulgur gives it a nice texture. It is good for sandwiches as well as toast.

450 g (1 lb) LOAF	INGREDIENTS	675 g (1½ lb) LOAF
4 tbsp	bulgur	6 tbsp
450 ml (16 fl oz)	water	450 ml (16 fl oz)
3 tbsp	milk	4½ tbsp
1 medium	cooked sweet potato, puréed	1 large
2 tbsp	butter	3 tbsp
2 tbsp	molasses	3 tbsp
1 tsp	salt	1½ tsp
130 g (5 oz)	bread flour	200 g (7½ oz)
130 g (5 oz)	wholewheat flour	200 g (7½ oz)
2 tsp	yeast	1 tbsp

METHOD

Put the bulgur wheat in a small pan with the water. Bring to the boil and let boil for 6 minutes. Remove from heat and drain. Let cool 15 minutes. Blot with kitchen paper to absorb excess moisture.

Put bulghur and remaining ingredients in bread tin in order suggested by your bread machine instructions. Set for wholewheat bread, medium crust. Press Start.

JALAPEÑO CHEESE BREAD

With one jalapeño chilli, this is a pleasantly spicy bread. With two jalapeños, it's hot but not scorching. The cheese flavour is more subtle, while the cornmeal gives it a finer texture.

450 g (1 lb) LOAF	INGREDIENTS	675 g (1½ lb) LOAF
40 g (1½ oz)	cornmeal	65 g (2½ oz)
65 ml (2½ fl oz)	boiling water	125 ml (4 fl oz)
125 ml (4 fl oz)	buttermilk	175 ml (6 fl oz)
1 tbsp	butter	1½ tbsp
1 tbsp	sugar	1½ tbsp
65 g (2½ oz)	grated Cheddar cheese	100 g (4 oz)
1 or 2	jalapeño chillies, chopped	2 or 3
3 tbsp	chopped fresh coriander	4½ tbsp
1 tsp	salt	1½ tsp
270 g (10 oz)	bread flour	425 g (15 oz)
1½ tsp	yeast	2¼ tsp

METHOD

Put the cornmeal in the bread machine tin. Add the boiling water, stir well. Let cool at least 10 minutes. Put remaining ingredients in bread tin in order suggested by your bread machine instructions. Set for white bread, medium crust. Press Start.

TIP

If you use freshly grated cheese, pack it tightly or much of the measurement will be air.

ONION CHEESE BREAD

*The onion and cheese flavours are not as strong as you might expect in this bread,
which makes good sandwiches.*

450 g (1 lb) LOAF	INGREDIENTS	675 g (1½ lb) LOAF
2 tbsp	water	3 tbsp
125 ml (4 fl oz)	milk	175 ml (6 fl oz)
1 tbsp	butter	1½ tbsp
1 tbsp	sugar	1½ tbsp
4	spring onions, thinly sliced	6
65 g (2½ oz)	shredded Swiss cheese	100 g (4 oz)
1 tsp	salt	1½ tsp
270 g (10 oz)	bread flour	425 g (15 oz)
1½ tsp	yeast	2¼ tsp

METHOD

Put ingredients in bread tin in order suggested by your
bread machine instructions. Set for white bread,
medium crust. Press Start.

TIP

If you use freshly grated cheese, pack it tightly or much
of the measurement will be air.

APPLE SAUCE OAT BRAN BREAD

This is a light bread with a delicate flavour and texture added by the oat bran and wheat germ. It makes excellent toast.

450 g (1 lb) LOAF	INGREDIENTS	675 g (1½ lb) LOAF
65 ml (2½ fl oz)	milk	125 ml (4 fl oz)
125 ml (4 fl oz)	unsweetened apple sauce	175 ml (6 fl oz)
1 tbsp	butter	1½ tbsp
2 tbsp	honey	3 tbsp
½ tsp	cinnamon	¾ tsp
¼ tsp	ground cloves	½ tsp
1 tsp	salt	1½ tsp
220 g (7¾ oz)	bread flour	365 g (12½ oz)
6 tbsp	oat bran	8 tbsp
2 tbsp	toasted wheat germ	3 tbsp
1½ tsp	yeast	2¼ tsp

METHOD

Put ingredients in bread tin in order suggested by your bread machine instructions. Set for white bread, medium crust. Press Start.

The amount of liquid needed may vary, depending on how watery the apple sauce is, so check the dough after it has been kneading for several minutes.

LEFT Apple Sauce Oat Bran Bread

CUBAN BREAD WITH YUCA

Yuca, also known as cassava, is a tuber whose potato-like flesh is widely used in the Caribbean. It is available in some ethnic markets. In this recipe, it adds density and subtle flavour. Plain mashed potatoes may be substituted for the yuca.

450 g (1 lb) LOAF	INGREDIENTS	675 g (1½ lb) LOAF
100 g (4 oz)	mashed yuca (see tip)	190 g (6½ oz)
125 ml (4 fl oz)	water	175 ml (6 fl oz)
1 tbsp	sugar	1½ tbsp
1 tsp	salt	1½ tsp
270 g (10 oz)	bread flour	425 g (15 oz)
1½ tsp	yeast	2¼ tsp
	several bay leaves	

METHOD

Put all ingredients except bay leaves in bread tin in order suggested by your bread machine instructions. Set for white bread, dough stage. Press Start.

When dough is ready, punch it down on a lightly floured board. Let it rest a few minutes. Then take it between your hands and roll it into a fat log, 25 go 30 cm (10 to 12 inches) long for the smaller loaf, 40 to 45 cm (15 to 18 inches) for the larger loaf. Put it on a baking sheet that has been sprinkled with cornmeal or in a buttered baguette mould. Cover and let rise 45 to 60 minutes. With a sharp knife, make several diagonal slashes, about a 1 cm (½ inch) deep, across the width of the loaf. Stick a bay leaf in each cut. Bake in a preheated 190°C/375°F/ Gas 5 oven until top is golden, about 30 to 40 minutes.

TIP

To cook yuca, quarter lengthwise. Remove fibrous core. Pare away dark peel and pink underlayer. Cut into chunks. Put in a large saucepan and cover with cold water. Add a pinch of salt, a splash of vinegar and two bay leaves. Bring to the boil, then reduce heat and simmer for about 30 minutes. Drain, cool and mash.

OATMEAL RAISIN BREAD

This is a hearty breakfast bread.

450 g (1 lb) LOAF	INGREDIENTS	675 g (1½ lb) LOAF
125 ml (4 fl oz)	very hot water	175 ml (6 fl oz)
40 g (1½ oz)	rolled oats	60 g (2½ oz)
125 ml (4 fl oz)	milk	175 ml (6 fl oz)
1 tbsp	butter	1½ tbsp
2 tbsp	brown sugar	3 tbsp
1 tsp	cinnamon	1½ tsp
1 tsp	salt	1½ tsp
220 g (7¾ oz)	bread flour	365 g (12½ oz)
2 tsp	yeast	1 tbsp
35 g (1½ oz)	raisins	50 g (2 oz)

METHOD

Put oats and hot water in bread machine tin and stir. Let sit at least 10 minutes.

Put remaining ingredients in bread tin in order suggested by your bread machine instructions. Set for white bread, medium crust. Press Start.

After about 15 minutes or when the beeper signals time to add fruit, add raisins.

PINEAPPLE ORANGE BRAN BREAD

This bread, which uses dried candied pineapple, is moist and slightly sweet.
It's good just plain. Use All-Bran or Fibre One, not bran flakes.

450 g (1 lb) LOAF	INGREDIENTS	675 g (1½ lb) LOAF
5 tbsp	water	125 ml (4 fl oz)
125 ml (4 fl oz)	milk	175 ml (6 fl oz)
1 tbsp	molasses	1½ tbsp
2 tbsp	butter	3 tbsp
1 tsp	grated orange zest	1½ tsp
1 tsp	salt	1½ tsp
35 g (1½ oz)	bran cereal	50 g (2 oz)
130 g (5 oz)	bread flour	200 g (7½ oz)
95 g (3½ oz)	wholewheat flour	225 g (8 oz)
1½ tsp	yeast	2¼ tsp
4 tbsp	chopped candied pineapple	6 tbsp

METHOD

Put all ingredients except pineapple in bread tin in order suggested by your bread machine instructions. Set for wholewheat bread, medium crust. Press Start. After about 15 minutes or when the beeper signals time to add fruit, add pineapple.

COCONUT DATE BREAD

Coconut, dates and nuts give this bread a tropical flavour.

450 g (1 lb) LOAF	INGREDIENTS	675 g (1½ lb) LOAF
1	egg	2
3 tbsp	water	2½ tbsp
65 ml (2½ fl oz)	milk	125 ml (4 fl oz)
1 tbsp	butter	1½ tbsp
2 tbsp	sugar	3 tbsp
1 tsp	ground allspice	1½ tsp
1 tsp	salt	1½ tsp
2 tbsp	wheat germ	3 tbsp
130 g (5 oz)	bread flour	200 g (7½ oz)
130 g (5 oz)	wholewheat flour	200 g (7½ oz)
1½ tsp	yeast	2¼ tsp
4 tbsp	chopped dates	6 tbsp
4 tbsp	sweetened flaked coconut	6 tbsp
4 tbsp	chopped macadamia nuts	6 tbsp

METHOD

Put all but the last three ingredients in bread tin in order suggested by your bread machine instructions. Set for wholewheat bread, medium crust. Press Start. After about 15 minutes or when the beeper signals time to add fruit, add the dates, coconut and nuts.

Pear Wholewheat Bread

This is a good wholewheat bread for breakfast, with a faint taste of pears, and texture added by the bulgur.

450 g (1 lb) LOAF	INGREDIENTS	675 g (1½ lb) LOAF
125 ml (4 fl oz)	puréed pear (see method)	175 ml (6 fl oz)
4 tbsp	bulgur	6 tbsp
450 ml (16 fl oz)	water	450 ml (16 fl oz)
5 tbsp	pear liquid (see method)	7½ tbsp
2 tbsp	powdered milk	3 tbsp
1 tbsp	butter	1½ tbsp
1 tbsp	honey	1½ tbsp
1 tsp	salt	1½ tsp
130 g (5 oz)	bread flour	200 g (7½ oz)
130 g (5 oz)	wholewheat flour	200 g (7½ oz)
2 tsp	yeast	1 tbsp

METHOD

Make the pear purée by peeling and coring 3 ripe pears for the smaller loaf, 4 or 5 pears for the larger one. Cut each pear into several pieces and put in a small saucepan with 1 or 2 tablespoons water. Start cooking over very low heat. The pears will quickly start releasing their own juices, and no more water will be needed. Increase to medium heat. Cook the pears, stirring frequently, until they are very soft. Then drain off as much liquid as you can, and save. If necessary, purée the pears in a blender or food processor, but mashing them with a fork may do the job. Then measure the amount needed in the recipe. Let cool.

Put the bulgur wheat in a small pan with 450 ml (16 fl oz) water. Bring to the boil and let boil for 6 minutes. Remove from heat and drain. Let cool 15 minutes. Blot with kitchen paper to absorb any excess moisture.

Put puréed pear, bulgur, measured pear liquid and remaining ingredients in bread tin in order suggested by your bread machine instructions. Set for wholewheat bread, medium crust. Press Start.

The stiffness of the dough may vary, depending on the liquid content of the cooked pears. Watch the dough while it is kneading and add a little flour, 1 tablespoon at a time, if it is too soft. Add water, 1 teaspoon at a time, if the dough is too stiff.

SWEET POTATO APPLE PECAN BREAD

This bread is slightly sweet, enhanced by the spices, dried apples and pecans in it. It is best toasted or plain with sweet butter, but would also be good for cream cheese sandwiches.

450 g (1 lb) LOAF	INGREDIENTS	675 g (1½ lb) LOAF
65 ml (2½ fl oz)	milk	125 ml (4 fl oz)
175 ml (6 fl oz)	puréed, cooked sweet potato	250 ml (8 fl oz)
2 tbsp	butter	3 tbsp
2 tbsp	honey	3 tbsp
1 tsp	salt	1½ tsp
½ tsp	cinnamon	¾ tsp
¼ tsp	ground cloves	¼ tsp
270 g (10 oz)	bread flour	425 g (15 oz)
1½ tsp	yeast	2¼ tsp
4 tbsp	chopped dried apples	6 tbsp
35 g (1¼ oz)	chopped pecans	55 g (1¾ oz)

METHOD

Put all ingredients except apples and nuts in bread tin in order suggested by your bread machine instructions. Set for white bread, medium crust. Press Start.

The stiffness of the dough may vary, depending on the liquid content of the sweet potato purée. Watch the dough while it is kneading and add a little flour, 1 tablespoon at a time, if it is too soft. Add water, 1 teaspoon at a time, if the dough is too stiff.

After about 15 minutes or when the beeper signals time to add fruit, add apples and pecans.

DATE-NUT WHEAT BREAD

*This is a dense bread with lots of texture added by the bulgur, dates and walnuts.
The dates also give it just a touch of sweetness. Use it for toast or with cream cheese.*

450 g (1 lb) LOAF	INGREDIENTS	675 g (1½ lb) LOAF
4 tbsp	bulgur	6 tbsp
500 ml (18 fl oz)	water	550 ml (20 fl oz)
65 ml (2½ fl oz)	milk	125 ml (4 fl oz)
1 tbsp	honey	1½ tbsp
2 tbsp	butter	3 tbsp
1 tsp	salt	1½ tsp
½ tsp	cinnamon	¾ tsp
130 g (5 oz)	wholewheat flour	200 g (7½ oz)
130 g (5 oz)	bread flour	200 g (7½ oz)
2 tsp	yeast	1 tbsp
35 g (1½ oz)	chopped dates	50 g (2 oz)
4 tbsp	chopped walnuts	6 tbsp

METHOD

Put the bulgur in a small pan with 450 ml (16 fl oz) water. Bring to the boil and let boil for 6 minutes. Remove from heat and drain. Let cool 15 minutes. Blot with kitchen paper to absorb excess moisture.

Put cooled bulgur, remaining water and all other ingredients except dates and walnuts in bread tin in order suggested by your bread machine instructions. Set for wholewheat bread, medium crust. Press Start. After about 15 minutes or when the beeper signals time to add fruit, add dates and walnuts.

APRICOT PECAN ANADAMA BREAD

*Anadama bread is an old New England hearth bread traditionally made with
cornmeal and molasses. This recipe dresses it up with dried apricots and pecans,
and makes a delicious breakfast or luncheon bread.*

450 g (1 lb) LOAF	INGREDIENTS	675 g (1½ lb) LOAF
125 ml (4 fl oz)	water	175 ml (6 fl oz)
4 tbsp	milk	6 tbsp
1 tbsp	butter	1½ tbsp
2 tbsp	molasses	3 tbsp
1 tsp	salt	1½ tsp
4 tbsp	cornmeal	6 tbsp
270 g (10 oz)	bread flour	425 g (15 oz)
1½ tsp	yeast	2¼ tsp
35 g (1½ oz)	chopped dried apricots	50 g (2 oz)
4 tbsp	chopped pecans	6 tbsp

METHOD

Put all ingredients except apricots and pecans in bread
tin in order suggested by your bread machine
instructions. Set for white bread, medium crust. Press
Start. After about 15 minutes or when the beeper signals
time to add fruit, add apricots and pecans.

SEMOLINA BREAD WITH COURGETTE AND MILLET

This is a light-textured white bread that is made slightly more crusty by the semolina flour, crunchy with millet and just a hint of courgette. Use it for sandwiches and toast.

450 g (1 lb) LOAF	INGREDIENTS	675 g (1½ lb) LOAF
125 ml (4 fl oz)	buttermilk	175 ml (6 fl oz)
2 tbsp	olive oil	3 tbsp
1 tbsp	sugar	1½ tbsp
1 small	raw courgette, grated	1 medium
½ tsp	baking soda	¾ tsp
2 tbsp	millet seed	3 tbsp
1 tsp	salt	1½ tsp
185 g (6½ oz)	bread flour	270 g (10 oz)
95 g (3½ oz)	semolina flour	130 g (5 oz)
1½ tsp	yeast	2¼ tsp

METHOD

Before starting the bread, blot the grated courgette on kitchen paper to absorb any excess moisture.

Put ingredients in bread tin in order suggested by your bread machine instructions. Set for white bread, medium crust. Press Start.

Check consistency of dough during kneading and add a little flour if needed.

APPLE-CRANBERRY GRAHAM BREAD

*Delicately flavoured with apple sauce and a hint of spice, balanced by the tang
of dried cranberries, this bread is given its soft but slightly chewy texture
by graham flour.*

450 g (1 lb) LOAF	INGREDIENTS	675 g (1½ lb) LOAF
65 ml (2½ fl oz)	water	125 ml (4 fl oz)
175 ml (6 fl oz)	unsweetened apple sauce	250 ml (8 fl oz)
1 tbsp	vegetable oil	1½ tbsp
1 tbsp	molasses	1½ tbsp
2 tbsp	powdered milk	3 tbsp
½ tsp	cinnamon	¾ tsp
½ tsp	ginger	¾ tsp
½ tsp	salt	¾ tsp
130 g (5 oz)	bread flour	200 g (7½ oz)
130 g (5 oz)	graham flour	200 g (7½ oz)
1½ tsp	yeast	2¼ tsp
40 g (1½ oz)	dried, sweetened cranberries	55 g (2 oz)

METHOD

Put ingredients except cranberries in bread tin in order suggested by your bread machine instructions. Set for wholewheat bread, medium crust. Press Start. After about 15 minutes of kneading or when the beeper signals time to add fruit, add cranberries.

The stiffness of the dough may vary, depending on the liquid content of the apple sauce. Watch the dough while it is kneading and add a little flour, 1 tablespoon at a time, if it is too soft. Add water, 1 teaspoon at a time, if the dough is too stiff.

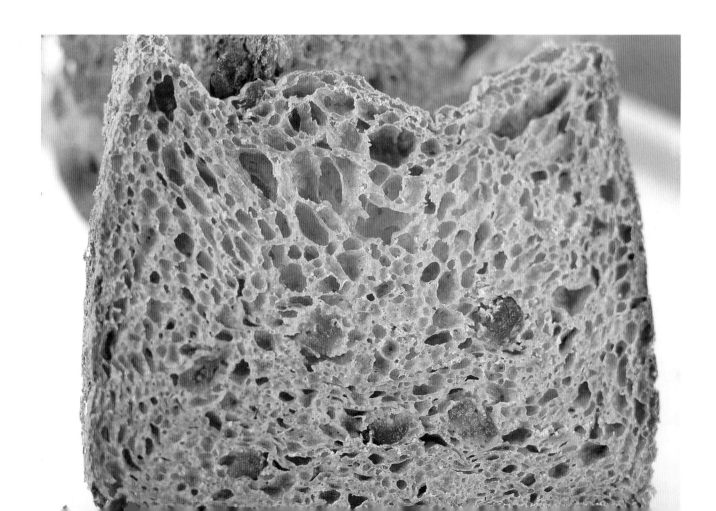

SWEET BREADS

Rich California Honey
Fig Bread   86

Date Walnut Pastries   87

Grandma's Cinnamon Raisin
Rolls   88

Tuscan Sweet Bread   89

California Fruit Braid   91

Zeppoles   92

Banana Nut Cinnamon Swirl   93

Norwegian Cardamom Bread   94

Apple Braid   95

Banana Date Monkey Bread   96

Scandinavian Tea Ring with
Apricot Cheese Filling   98

Prune Yoghurt Breakfast
Crescents   99

RICH CALIFORNIA HONEY FIG BREAD

*This is a sweet bread, flavoured with figs, rum, vanilla and honey. Because
of the high sugar content, it tends to scorch in the bread machine and should be
baked in the oven. The figs should marinate in the rum at least 30 minutes
or as long as overnight.*

450 g (1 lb) LOAF	INGREDIENTS	675 g (1½ lb) LOAF
2 tbsp	rum	3 tbsp
35 g (1½ oz)	coarsely chopped figs	50 g (2 oz)
1	egg	1 + 1 yolk
125 ml (4 fl oz)	milk	175 ml (6 fl oz)
1 tsp	vanilla extract	1½ tsp
1 tbsp	butter	1½ tbsp
2 tbsp	honey	3 tbsp
½ tsp	salt	¾ tsp
270 g (10 oz)	bread flour	425 g (15 oz)
1½ tsp	yeast	2¼ tsp

METHOD

Pour the rum over the chopped figs and set aside to
marinate at least 30 minutes.

Put figs and remaining ingredients in bread tin in order
suggested by your bread machine instructions. Set for
dough. Press Start.

When dough is ready, punch it down on a lightly
floured board. Let it rest a few minutes. Butter a
25-cm (9½-inch) loaf tin (tin can be smaller for the
smaller recipe). Shape the dough into a loaf and put it
in the pan, turning so all sides are buttered. Cover and
let rise in a warm place for 1 hour.

When bread has risen, bake it in a preheated
180°C/350°F/Gas 4 oven for about 30 to 45 minutes.

DATE WALNUT PASTRIES

This recipe makes yeast turnovers with a tangy date-walnut filling.

MAKES 10	INGREDIENTS	MAKES 15
	DOUGH	
150 ml (5 fl oz)	milk	250 ml (5 fl oz)
4 tbsp	brown sugar	6 tbsp
4 tbsp	butter	6 tbsp
½ tsp	salt	¾ tsp
270 g (10 oz)	bread flour	425 g (15 oz)
1½ tsp	yeast	2¼ tsp
	FILLING	
2 tbsp	butter	3 tbsp
35 g (1¼ oz)	plain or bread flour	50 g (2 oz)
2 tbsp	brown sugar	3 tbsp
½ tsp	cinnamon	¾ tsp
4 tbsp	chopped walnuts	6 tbsp
45 g (1½ oz)	chopped dates	60 g (2¼ oz)
	TOPPING	
2 tbsp	milk	3 tbsp
1 tbsp	sugar	1½ tbsp
¼ tsp	cinnamon	½ tsp

METHOD

Put dough ingredients in bread tin in order suggested by your bread machine instructions. Set for white bread, dough stage. Press Start.

While dough is rising, make filling. Melt butter in small frying pan. Add flour, sugar and cinnamon and stir until it forms a paste. Remove from heat and stir in walnuts and dates. Let cool.

Butter one or two baking sheets.

When dough is ready, remove from bread tin and punch down on floured surface. The dough will be soft and sticky. Roll into a thick log and cut into 10 pieces for the smaller recipe, 15 pieces for the larger recipe. Roll each piece into an oval 3 mm (⅛ inch) thick. Put some of the filling on half of each oval, fold the other half over and pinch each turnover closed. Place on the baking sheets. Lightly brush the top of each turnover with milk. Combine the cinnamon and sugar and sprinkle over the top of the pastries. Put in a warm place to rise for 1 hour.

Bake in a preheated 180°C/350°F/Gas 4 oven until golden brown, for 20 to 25 minutes.

GRANDMA'S CINNAMON RAISIN ROLLS

My grandmother, Letty Belden, has made these delicious rolls by hand in huge batches for years. She gladly shared her recipe, which I have cut down in size and converted for use in a bread machine.

MAKES 12	INGREDIENTS	MAKES 18
1	egg	1 + 1 yolk
50 g (1¾ oz)	mashed potatoes	95 g (3¾ oz)
3 tbsp	milk	4½ tbsp
3 tbsp	butter	4½ tbsp
3 tbsp	sugar	4½ tbsp
½ tsp	salt	¾ tsp
½ tsp	baking powder	¾ tsp
¼ tsp	baking soda	½ tsp
270 g (10 oz)	bread flour	425 g (15 oz)
1½ tsp	yeast	2¼ tsp
2 tbsp	very soft butter	3 tbsp
3 tbsp	brown sugar	4½ tbsp
1 tsp	cinnamon	1½ tsp
45 g (1½ oz)	raisins	50 g (2 oz)

	ICING	
130 g (5 oz)	icing sugar	200 g (7½ oz)
1 tbsp	milk	1½ tbsp
¼ tsp	vanilla extract	½ tsp

METHOD

Put all but the last four dough ingredients in bread tin in order suggested by your bread machine instructions. Set for white bread, dough stage. Press Start.

When dough is ready, punch it down on a lightly floured board. Let it rest a few minutes, then roll it out into a rectangle about 25 x 40 cm (10 x 15 inches) for the smaller recipe, about 40 x 40 cm (15 x 15 inches) for the larger one. Spread the soft butter over the dough. Mix the brown sugar and cinnamon and sprinkle over the dough. Sprinkle the raisins over the sugar.

Starting at a long end, roll the dough into a tight cylinder. Trim the uneven ends. Cut into 20-mm (¾-inch) slices. Place slightly apart on one or two buttered baking sheets. Cover, put in a warm place and let rise until doubled in bulk, about 1 hour.

With your fingertip, gently press any exposed raisins back into folds of dough. Bake rolls in a preheated 180°C/350°F/Gas 4 oven until golden brown, 20 to 25 minutes. While rolls are still warm, make icing by mixing icing sugar, milk and vanilla. Spread icing over the tops of rolls and allow some to drip down sides.

NOTE

This recipe is based on pure mashed potatoes with no additions. If milk or other liquids have been added to the potatoes, check during kneading and add a little flour if dough is too wet.

TUSCAN SWEET BREAD

This crusty oven-baked bread brings together a delicious mélange of orange, rum and fennel. It is good for breakfast or tea. Baked in a ring and decoratively slashed, it makes a pretty centrepiece.

450 g (1 lb) LOAF	INGREDIENTS	675 g (1½ lb) LOAF
1	egg	1 + 1 yolk
3 tbsp	milk	4½ tbsp
4 tbsp	water	6 tbsp
1 tsp	rum	1½ tsp
2 tbsp	butter	3 tbsp
3 tbsp	sugar	4½ tbsp
1 tsp	grated orange zest	1½ tsp
1 tsp	fennel seeds	1½ tsp
1 tsp	salt	1½ tsp
185 g (6½ oz)	bread flour	270 g (10 oz)
95 g (3½ oz)	semolina flour	130 g (5 oz)
1½ tsp	yeast	2¼ tsp
3 tbsp	golden raisins	4½ tbsp

TOPPING

1 egg yolk
1 tsp rum
1½–2 tsp sugar

METHOD

Put all dough ingredients except raisins in bread tin in order suggested by your bread machine instructions. Set for dough. Press Start. After about 15 minutes or when the beeper signals time to add fruit, add raisins.

When dough is ready, punch it down on a lightly floured board. Let it rest a few minutes. Then take it between your hands and roll it into a rope, about 40 cm (15 inches) long for the smaller loaf, 45 to 50 cm (18 to 20 inches) for the larger. Put it on a lightly buttered baking sheet. Bring the ends together to form a circle. Cover and let rise 45 to 60 minutes.

Lightly beat the egg yolk and rum. Paint onto the top of the bread and sprinkle with sugar. Cut diagonal slashes about 5 cm (2 inches) apart in the top. Bake in a preheated 180°C/350°F/Gas 4 oven for 35 to 55 minutes.

California Fruit Braid

Filled with dates, figs and dried apricots, this bread has a natural sweetness.
Twisted into a plait, it makes an impressive appearance at a brunch or luncheon.

450 g (1 lb) LOAF	INGREDIENTS	675 g (1½ lb) LOAF
65 ml (2½ fl oz)	water	125 ml (4 fl oz)
65 ml (2½ fl oz)	milk	125 ml (4 fl oz)
2 tbsp	butter	3 tbsp
2 tbsp	brown sugar	3 tbsp
½ tsp	ground nutmeg	¾ tsp
1 tsp	grated orange zest	1½ tsp
1 tsp	salt	1½ tsp
270 g (10 oz)	bread flour	425 g (15 oz)
1½ tsp	yeast	2¼ tsp
3 tbsp	chopped dried apricots	4½ tbsp
3 tbsp	chopped dates	4½ tbsp
3 tbsp	chopped figs	4½ tbsp

TOPPING

1 egg, beaten with a fork
1 tsp water
1–2 tbsp sugar

METHOD

Put all dough ingredients except fruits in bread tin in order suggested by your bread machine instructions. Set for dough. Press Start. After about 15 minutes or when the beeper signals time to add fruit, add apricots, dates and figs.

When dough is ready, punch it down on a lightly floured board. Let it rest a few minutes, then cut it into three equal pieces. Take each piece between your hands and roll it into a rope, about 40 cm (15 inches) long for the smaller loaf, 45 to 50 cm (18 to 20 inches) for the larger. Lay the three ropes on a non-stick or lightly buttered baking sheet.

Beginning at one end, pinch the ends together and plait the three ropes, then pinch the bottom ends together. Make a wash of the egg and water and brush it over the bread. Sprinkle lightly with sugar. Cover and let rise until bread has doubled in bulk, 45 to 60 minutes.

Place in a preheated 190°C/375°F/Gas 5 oven and bake until the top is golden brown, about 30 to 45 minutes.

ZEPPOLES

Zeppoles, also called zappla, are Italian doughnuts: small circles of fried dough.
For variety, add a pinch of grated lemon zest or a dash or nutmeg – or both.

MAKES 16	INGREDIENTS	MAKES 24
1	egg	2
50 ml (2 fl oz)	water	50 ml (2 fl oz)
85 ml (3 fl oz)	milk	120 ml (4 fl oz)
1 tsp	vanilla extract	1½ tsp
1 tbsp	butter	1½ tbsp
1 tbsp	sugar	1½ tbsp
½ tsp	salt	¾ tsp
270 g (10 oz)	bread flour	425 g (15 oz)
1½ tsp	yeast	2¼ tsp

vegetable oil for frying
icing sugar

METHOD

Put all ingredients except oil and confectioner's sugar in bread tin in order suggested by your bread machine instructions. Set for dough. Press Start.

Lightly butter one or two baking sheets. When dough is ready, remove from bread tin, punch down on lightly floured surface and let rest a few minutes. Roll the dough into a fat log. Cut into 16 pieces for the smaller recipe, 24 pieces for the larger recipe. Roll each piece into a ball and flatten slightly. With thumb and forefinger, pinch the centre of the circle until dough tears. Put finger through hole and stretch open. Place the circles on the baking sheets. Put in a warm place and let rise for 40 minutes.

When risen, pour 5 to 7 cm (2 to 3 inches) of oil into a wide saucepan and heat oil to 180°C (360°F), using a thermometer. Carefully remove several zeppoles from the baking sheet and drop into the hot oil. Zeppoles should not crowd each other. Cook for one minute, then turn each zeppole. Cook another minute or until both sides are golden brown. Remove, drain and place on kitchen paper. Make sure oil has remained at 180°C (360°F); lower or raise heat as needed. Add several more zeppoles and continue until all zeppoles are cooked.

Put some icing sugar in a paper bag. Add zeppoles one or two at a time and shake to coat them with sugar. Knock off excess sugar.

These are best served warm. They can be kept in a warm oven while the others are cooking.

BANANA NUT CINNAMON SWIRL

Banana is mixed into the dough of this breakfast bread. Before baking, the dough is rolled out, spread with butter, sprinkled with cinnamon, brown sugar, and pecans, and rolled up. When it's baked, it's similar to a not overly sweet cinnamon roll.

450 g (1 lb) LOAF	INGREDIENTS	675 g (1½ lb) LOAF
1	egg	2
2 tbsp	milk	2 tbsp
60 g (2½ oz)	mashed ripe banana	100 g (4 oz)
1 tbsp	butter	1½ tbsp
1 tbsp	sugar	1½ tbsp
1 tsp	salt	1½ tsp
270 g (10 oz)	bread flour	425 g (15 oz)
1½ tsp	yeast	2¼ tsp
	FILLING	
1 tbsp	very soft butter	1½ tbsp
2 tbsp	brown sugar	3 tbsp
½ tsp	cinnamon	¾ tsp
2 tbsp	chopped pecans	3 tbsp

METHOD

Put dough ingredients in bread tin in order suggested by your bread machine instructions. Set for white bread, dough stage. Press Start.

When dough is ready, punch it down on a lightly floured board. Let it rest a few minutes, then roll it out into an oval no more than 23 cm (9 inches) wide, or the length of your loaf pan. Spread the butter over the dough. Mix the brown sugar and cinnamon and sprinkle over the dough. Sprinkle the pecans over the sugar.

Roll the dough into a tight cylinder. Put the cylinder, down, into a buttered 25-cm (9½-inch) loaf tin (tin can be smaller for the smaller recipe). Rub some additional butter into the top of the loaf. Cover, put in a warm place and let rise for 1 hour.

When bread has risen, bake in a preheated 180°C/350°F/ Gas 4 oven until the top is golden brown, about 30 to 45 minutes.

NORWEGIAN CARDAMOM BREAD

Fresh cardamom seeds are a delicious addition to a sweet bread and are particularly popular in Scandinavian countries. Whole seedpods can sometimes be found in the spice racks of well-stocked grocery stores. Break open the pods, remove the tiny black seeds and grind them in a grinder or mortar and pestle. Fresh cardamom is hard to find, and we usually must be satisfied with the milder flavour of dried, ground cardamom. Here, we use it in a plaited wholewheat bread that is full of sultanas, dried apricots and almonds.

450 g (1 lb) LOAF	INGREDIENTS	675 g (1½ lb) LOAF
1	egg	2
6 tbsp	milk	7 tbsp
2 tbsp	vegetable oil	3 tbsp
2 tbsp	honey	3 tbsp
1 tsp	salt	1½ tsp
1 tsp	ground cardamom	1½ tsp
95 g (3½ oz)	wholewheat flour	130 g (5 oz)
185 g (6½ oz)	bread flour	270 g (10 oz)
2 tsp	yeast	1 tbsp
4 tbsp	chopped dried apricots	6 tbsp
4 tbsp	sultanas	6 tbsp
4 tbsp	slivered almonds	6 tbsp

EGG WASH

1 egg, beaten with a fork

2 tsp water

METHOD

Put all dough ingredients except apricots, sultanas and almonds in bread tin in order suggested by your bread machine instructions. Set for wholewheat dough. Press Start. After about 15 minutes or when the beeper signals time to add fruit, add sultanas, apricots and nuts.

When dough is ready, punch it down on a lightly floured board. Let it rest a few minutes, then cut it into three equal pieces. Take each piece between your hands and roll it into a rope, about 40 cm (15 inches) long for the smaller loaf, 45 to 50 cm (18 to 20 inches) for the larger. Lay the three ropes on a non-stick or lightly buttered baking sheet. Beginning at one end, pinch the ends together and plait the three ropes, then pinch the bottom ends together. Make a wash of the egg and water and brush it over the bread. Cover and let rise until bread has doubled in bulk, 45 to 60 minutes.

Place in a preheated 190°C/375°F/Gas 5 oven and bake until the top is golden brown, 25 to 40 minutes.

APPLE BRAID

This luscious cake is pretty and smells like apple pie. It can be filled and plaited, then left in the refrigerator overnight. In the morning, bring to room temperature, let rise and bake. My favourite apples for the filling are green Pippins or Granny Smiths, but other apples can be used.

450 g (1 lb) LOAF	INGREDIENTS	675 g (1½ lb) LOAF
125 ml (4 fl oz)	milk	175 ml (6 fl oz)
1	egg	2
3 tbsp	butter	4½ tbsp
4 tbsp	sugar	6 tbsp
½ tsp	salt	¾ tsp
270 g (10 oz)	bread flour	425 g (15 oz)
2 tsp	yeast	1 tbsp
2 tbsp	icing sugar	3 tbsp
	FILLING	
1½	apples	2
1 tsp	flour	1½ tsp
2 tbsp	sugar	3 tbsp
½ tsp	cinnamon	¾ tsp
½ tsp	vanilla extract	¾ tsp
½ tsp	lemon juice	¾ tsp
2 tbsp	raisins	3 tbsp

METHOD

Put all dough ingredients except icing sugar in bread tin in order suggested by your bread machine instructions. Set for white bread, dough stage. Press Start.

While dough is rising, prepare the filling. Peel, core and chop the apples into 6-mm (¼-inch) dice. Toss with remaining ingredients.

When dough is ready, punch it down on a lightly floured board. Let it rest a few minutes. Butter a large baking sheet. Roll out the dough into a rectangle, 8 mm (⅓ inch) thick, and place on the baking sheet. With the dull side of a knife blade, mark – but do not cut – the rectangle into thirds. Spread the filling along the middle third.

Use the knife to cut the outer thirds diagonally into strips 2.5 cm (1 inch) wide. Bring up the two ends of the middle third just slightly to form an edge, then at either end, cross the two strips on either side over the middle. Working from one end of the plait to the other, cross alternating strips over the middle.

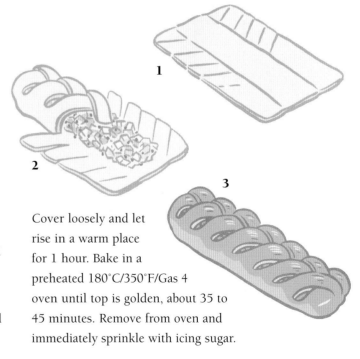

Cover loosely and let rise in a warm place for 1 hour. Bake in a preheated 180°C/350°F/Gas 4 oven until top is golden, about 35 to 45 minutes. Remove from oven and immediately sprinkle with icing sugar.

BANANA DATE MONKEY BREAD

This is a very sweet pull-apart bread, loved by children, and
delicious for breakfast.

450 g (1 lb) LOAF	INGREDIENTS	675 g (1½ lb) LOAF
125 ml (4 fl oz)	plain yoghurt	185 ml (7 fl oz)
half	banana, mashed	whole
25 g (1 oz)	chopped dates	25 g (1 oz)
1 tbsp	water	1½ tbsp
2 tbsp	butter	3 tbsp
2 tbsp	honey	3 tbsp
½ tsp	salt	¾ tsp
½ tsp	ground nutmeg	¾ tsp
260 g (9 oz)	bread flour	400 g (14 oz)
1½ tsp	yeast	2¼ tsp
	DIPPING	
2 tbsp	rum (see below)	3 tbsp
3 tbsp	melted butter	4½ tbsp
100 g (3½ oz)	sugar	125 g (4½ oz)
80 g (3 oz)	brown sugar	125 g (4½ oz)
80 g (3 oz)	cinnamon	¾ tsp
½ tsp	ground nutmeg	¾ tsp

METHOD

Put dough ingredients in bread tin in order suggested by your bread machine instructions. Set for white bread, dough stage. Press Start.

Lightly butter a baking dish. A 25-cm (10-inch) Bundt tin or tube tin works well for both sizes, or use a round casserole dish. Stir the rum or other flavouring into the melted butter. In another bowl, mix the sugars, cinnamon and nutmeg, then put about half the sugar mixture in a separate bowl.

When dough is ready, punch down. Roll dough into a thick log and cut into 24 pieces for the smaller loaf, 30 to 36 pieces for the larger loaf. Roll each piece into a ball; it does not need to be perfectly round. Dip each ball in butter-rum mix, then in sugar mix. As the butter drips into the sugar mix, it will become difficult to work with, so add a little sugar mix from the reserve bowl. Layer the sugared balls into the baking pan so they are close but not touching; they need room to rise. With each succeeding layer, place balls so they overlap empty spaces below. When the dough is layered, pour any remaining butter-rum mix and sugar over the loaf.

Cover the baking pan loosely and put it in a warm place to rise until doubled in volume, about 45 minutes. Or at this point you can put the assembled loaf in the refrigerator, where it will rise very slowly. The next morning, or when you are ready to bake, let loaf return to room temperature and finish rising.

Bake in a preheated 180°C/350°F/Gas 4 oven until bread is lightly browned and a skewer inserted in the bread comes out clean, 25 to 40 minutes. Invert bread on to a serving plate, being very careful of any hot syrup that has collected in the bottom of the pan. Let cool just long enough that the sugar syrup is not burning hot, and serve.

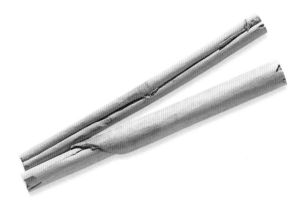

TIP

You may substitute rum flavouring, vanilla essence or orange juice for the rum.

Scandinavian Tea Ring
with Apricot Cheese Filling

This pretty coffee-time cake uses a sweet egg dough flavoured with cardamom, preferably freshly ground. It is filled with a mixture of dried apricots and cream cheese.

450 g (1 lb) LOAF	INGREDIENTS	675 g (1½ lb) LOAF
1	egg	2
120 ml (4 fl oz)	milk	175 ml (6 fl oz)
3 tbsp	butter	4½ tbsp
2 tbsp	sugar	3 tbsp
1 tsp	ground cardamom	1½ tsp
1 tsp	salt	1½ tsp
270 g (10 oz)	bread flour	425 g (15 oz)
1½ tsp	yeast	2¼ tsp

	FILLING	
200 g (8 oz)	cream cheese, at room temperature	350 g (12 oz)
1	egg yolk	1
2 tbsp	sugar	3 tbsp
1 tsp	vanilla essence	1½ tsp
½ tsp	grated lemon zest	¾ tsp
½ tsp	ground cardamom	¾ tsp
50 g (1¾ oz)	chopped dried apricots	65 g (2½ oz)

METHOD

Put dough ingredients in bread tin in order suggested by your bread machine instructions. Set for white bread, dough stage. Press Start.

While dough is rising, make the filling. Beat together the cream cheese and egg. Add sugar, vanilla, lemon and cardamom and mix well. Add apricots. Do not refrigerate – the filling needs to be soft.

When dough is ready, punch it down on a lightly floured board. Let it rest a few minutes. Then roll it out into a rectangle about 25 x 40 cm (10 x 15 inches) for the smaller recipe, about 40 x 40 cm (15 x 15 inches) for the larger one. Spread the filling over the dough. Starting at a long end, roll the dough into a tight cylinder. Place the cylinder on a buttered baking sheet. Pull the ends together to form a circle. With a sharp knife, make cuts in the outside of the ring every 20 mm (¾ inch), cutting about halfway through the dough. Do not slice all the way through. Cover, put in a warm place and let rise until doubled in bulk, about 1 hour.

1

2

3

Bake tea ring in a preheated 180°C/350°F/Gas 4 oven until golden brown, 25 to 35 minutes.

4

PRUNE YOGHURT BREAKFAST CRESCENTS

Prunes give the dough of these breakfast treats sweetness and moisture. The chopped prunes are added at the beginning so that they are puréed during the kneading and are well incorporated into the dough.

MAKES 16	INGREDIENTS	MAKES 24
175 ml (6 fl oz)	plain yoghurt	250 ml (8 fl oz)
1	egg	1 + 1 yolk
70 g (2¼ oz)	chopped dried prunes	90 g (3½ oz)
2 tbsp	butter	3 tbsp
2 tbsp	sugar	3 tbsp
1 tsp	salt	1½ tsp
270 g (10 oz)	bread flour	425 g (15 oz)
1½ tsp	yeast	2¼ tsp

	FILLING	
2 tbsp	very soft butter	3 tbsp
55 g (1¾ oz)	brown sugar	65 g (2½ oz)
1 tsp	cinnamon	1½ tsp
55 g (1¾ oz)	finely chopped pecans	65 g (2½ oz)

METHOD

Put dough ingredients in bread tin in order suggested by your bread machine instructions. Set for white bread, dough stage. Press Start.

When dough is ready, punch it down on a lightly floured board. Cut the smaller recipe into two equal pieces, the larger recipe into three. Let it rest a few minutes. Butter two baking sheets, then roll each piece into a circle about 20 cm (8 inches) in diameter. Spread the soft butter over the dough. Mix the brown sugar and cinnamon and sprinkle over the butter. Sprinkle the pecans over the sugar.

Cut each circle into 8 wedges. Starting from the outside of the circle, loosely roll up each wedge, working towards the point. Stretch slightly and pull into a curve. Set each croissant on baking sheet, with the point underneath.

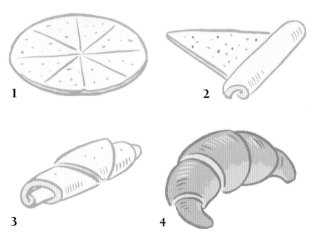

Cover, put in a warm place and let rise until doubled in size, about 1 hour. Bake in a preheated 190°C/375°F/ Gas 5 oven for 12 to 15 minutes.

OVEN-BAKED BREADS

Spinach Cheese Swirl   101

Foccacio with Olives and
Sun-dried Tomatoes   102

Coriander Pesto Bread   103

Savoury Kugelhopf   104

Wholewheat Pesto Foccacio   105

Fougasse   106

Braided Brioche   107

Tuscan Sage Wholewheat
Bread   109

Italian Sausage Bread   110

SPINACH CHEESE SWIRL

A tender, flavourful wholewheat dough is wrapped around a savoury filling of ricotta cheese, spinach, onions and thyme. Try this with meatloaf sandwiches or as a hearty accompaniment to soup or salad.

450 g (1 lb) LOAF	INGREDIENTS	675 g (1½ lb) LOAF
75 g (3 oz)	mashed potatoes	115 g (4½ oz)
120 ml (4 fl oz)	milk	175 ml (5 fl oz)
2 tbsp	butter	3 tbsp
1 tbsp	sugar	1½ tbsp
½ tsp	dried thyme	¾ tsp
1 tsp	salt	1½ tsp
175 g (6 oz)	bread flour	270 g (10 oz)
75 g (3 oz)	wholewheat flour	150 g (5 oz)
1½ tsp	yeast	2¼ tsp

	FILLING	
65 g (2¼ oz)	ricotta cheese	90 g (3½ oz)
50 g (2 oz)	chopped cooked spinach	75 g (3 oz)
1 tsp	olive oil	1½ tsp
3 tbsp	chopped onion	4½ tbsp
½ tsp	salt	¾ tsp
¼ tsp	pepper	½ tsp
¼ tsp	dried thyme	½ tsp

METHOD

Put dough ingredients in bread tin in order suggested by your bread machine instructions. Set for wholewheat bread, dough stage. Press Start.

When dough is working, make the filling. Start immediately, because the spinach and ricotta must have time to drain completely. Put the spinach and ricotta in separate colanders to let them drain, at least 30 minutes. Stir once or twice to release liquids. Squeeze the spinach by hand to remove additional water and press between a double thickness of kitchen paper.

Heat the olive oil in a small frying pan and sauté the onions for 5 minutes. Remove from heat and let cool slightly. Then combine the spinach, cheese, onion and seasonings.

When dough is ready, punch it down on a lightly floured board. Let it rest a few minutes. Butter a 25-cm (9½-inch) loaf tin (can be smaller for smaller loaf). Roll the dough out into a rectangle no wider than the length of the bread tin. Gently spread the spinach-cheese filling over the surface of the bread, taking care not to tear the dough. Starting at the short end, roll dough into a cylinder. Put the dough into the bread tin, seam side down. Cover and let rise in a warm place for 1 hour.

Bake in a preheated 180°C/350°F/Gas 4 oven until golden, about 35 to 40 minutes.

NOTE

This recipe is based on pure mashed potatoes with no additions. If milk or other liquids have been added to the potatoes, check during kneading and add a little flour if dough is too wet.

FOCCACIO WITH OLIVES AND SUN-DRIED TOMATOES

This foccacio is full of flavour and is best served plain. It should be eaten hot from the oven.

450 g (1 lb) LOAF	INGREDIENTS	675 g (1½ lb) LOAF
175 ml (6 fl oz)	water	250 ml (8 fl oz)
2 tbsp	olive oil	3 tbsp
1 tsp	salt	1½ tsp
¼ tsp	dried thyme	½ tsp
½ tsp	dried oregano	¾ tsp
270 g (10 oz)	bread flour	425 g (15 oz)
1¼ tsp	yeast	2 tsp
4 tbsp	chopped sun-dried tomatoes	6 tbsp
4 tbsp	kalamata olives, coarsely chopped	6 tbsp
2 tbsp	olive oil	3 tbsp
4 tbsp	grated Asiago cheese	6 tbsp

METHOD

Put first seven ingredients in bread tin in order suggested by your bread machine instructions. Set for dough stage. Press Start. After about 15 minutes or when the beeper signals time to add fruit, add tomatoes and olives.

When dough is ready, punch it down on a lightly floured board. Let it rest a few minutes, then roll it into a round about 1 cm (½ inch) thick. Sprinkle cornmeal on a baking sheet. Put the dough on the baking sheet. Spread remaining olive oil over the top and sprinkle with the cheese. Bake bread in a preheated 200°C/400°F/ Gas 6 oven until lightly browned, about 20 minutes.

CORIANDER PESTO BREAD

A spicy filling of coriander pesto with ricotta cheese and jalapeño chilli gives this egg bread a deliciously different character. It goes well with grilled meat or spicy soup and is also good on its own.

450 g (1 lb) LOAF	INGREDIENTS	675 g (1½ lb) LOAF
120 ml (4 fl oz)	milk	175 ml (6 fl oz)
1	egg	2
2 tbsp	butter	3 tbsp
1 tbsp	sugar	1½ tbsp
1 small	jalapeño chilli, chopped fine	1 large
1 tsp	salt	1½ tsp
270 g (10 oz)	bread flour	425 g (15 oz)
1½ tsp	yeast	2¼ tsp

	FILLING	
75 g (3 oz)	ricotta cheese	115 g (4½ oz)
4 tbsp	fresh coriander, tightly packed	6 tbsp
1	clove garlic, chopped	1½ cloves
2 tbsp	chopped walnuts	3 tbsp
½ small	jalapeño chilli, chopped	1 small
1 tsp	olive oil	1½ tsp
½ tsp	salt	¾ tsp
¼ tsp	fresh-ground black pepper	½ tsp

METHOD

Put dough ingredients in bread tin in order suggested by your bread machine instructions. Set for white bread, dough stage. Press Start.

While the dough is working, make the filling. Start immediately as the ricotta must have time to drain completely. Put the ricotta in a colander to let it drain, at least 30 minutes. Stir once or twice to release liquids.

While ricotta is draining, put the remaining filling ingredients in a food processor or blender and process until a coarse paste forms. Do not allow the paste to become too smooth. When the ricotta is thoroughly drained, stir in the pesto.

When dough is ready, punch it down on a lightly floured board. Let it rest a few minutes. Butter a 25-cm (9½-inch) loaf pan (can be smaller for smaller loaf). Roll the dough out into a rectangle no wider than the length of the bread tin. Gently spread the filling over the surface of the bread, taking care not to tear the dough. Starting at the short end, roll dough into a cylinder. If necessary, turn ends under. Put the dough into the bread tin, seam side down. Cover and let rise in a warm place for 1 hour.

Bake in a preheated 180°C/350°F/Gas 4 oven until golden, about 35 to 40 minutes.

TIP

Most of the heat in a jalapeño chilli is in the inner membrane. For a milder bread, remove the seeds and membranes.

SAVOURY KUGELHOPF

The kugelhopf is a rich Austrian bread for special occasions. Traditionally it is a sweet bread loaded with fruit, but this version is a savoury bread, made with bacon, cheese and onions. Eat it as an accompaniment to soup and salad. Made with extra egg and butter, it cannot be baked in the bread machine. The kugelhopf has its own special tin, but can be baked in a Bundt tin or tube tin.

450 g (1 lb) LOAF	INGREDIENTS	675 g (1½ lb) LOAF
2 + 1 yolk	eggs	4
120 ml (4 fl oz)	milk	65 ml (2½ fl oz)
4 tbsp	butter	6 tbsp
1 tbsp	sugar	1½ tbsp
½ tsp	dried thyme	¾ tsp
¼ tsp	freshly ground black pepper	½ tsp
1 tsp	salt	1½ tsp
270 g (10 oz)	bread flour	425 g (15 oz)
2 tsp	yeast	1 tbsp
4 slices	bacon	6 slices
25 g (1 oz)	chopped onion	40 g (1½ oz)
25 g (1 oz)	shredded Swiss cheese	40 g (1½ oz)

METHOD

Put all but last three ingredients in bread tin in order suggested by your bread machine instructions. Set wheat dough. Press Start.

Meanwhile, dice the bacon and cook until crisp. Remove bacon, drain on kitchen paper, and let cool. Pour off all but a few teaspoons of bacon fat. Reheat the fat and add the onion. Sauté for 10 minutes. Remove from heat, drain, and let cool.

Butter a 25-cm (10-inch) tube tin for either size loaf, or a smaller tin can be used for the smaller loaf.

When dough is ready, remove from bread machine, punch down on a lightly floured surface, then let rest a few minutes. Gradually knead in the bacon, onions and cheese. Roll dough between your hands to make a thick log and put it in the tin, stretching or shaping as needed. Cover and put in a warm place to rise for 45 minutes.

Bake Kugelhopf in a preheated 180°C/350°F/Gas 4 oven until golden brown, about 35 to 45 minutes.

WHOLEWHEAT PESTO FOCCACIO

This simple flatbread should be eaten warm. It can be served plain or dipped in a high-quality extra-virgin olive oil.

450 g (1 lb) LOAF	INGREDIENTS	675 g (1½ lb) LOAF
175 ml (6 fl oz)	water	250 ml (8 fl oz)
2 tbsp	olive oil	3 tbsp
1 tsp	salt	1½ tsp
130 g (5 oz)	bread flour	200 g (7½ oz)
130 g (5 oz)	wholewheat flour	200 g (7½ oz)
1¼ tsp	yeast	2 tsp
4 tbsp	prepared pesto	6 tbsp
2 tbsp	pine nuts or chopped walnuts	3 tbsp

METHOD

Put all but the last two ingredients in bread tin in order suggested by your bread machine instructions. Set for wholewheat dough. Press Start.

When dough is ready, punch it down on a lightly floured board. Let it rest a few minutes, then roll it into a round about 1 cm (½ inch) thick. Sprinkle cornmeal on a baking sheet. Put the dough on the baking sheet. Spread the pesto over the top and sprinkle nuts over pesto. Bake bread in a preheated 200°C/400°F/Gas 6 oven until lightly browned, about 20 minutes.

FOUGASSE

Fougasse is a flatbread made in southern France that is similar to foccacio but is cut prior to baking. This recipe is more elaborate than a basic fougasse. It is a good starter or an accompaniment to soup or salad.

450 g (1 lb) LOAF	INGREDIENTS	675 g (1½ lb) LOAF
2 slices	bacon	3 slices
175 ml (6 fl oz)	water	250 ml (8 fl oz)
2 tbsp	olive oil	3 tbsp
2 tsp	sugar	1 tbsp
1 tsp	salt	1½ tsp
1 tsp	finely chopped rosemary, fresh or dry	1½ tsp
270 g (10 oz)	bread flour	425 g (15 oz)
1½ tsp	yeast	2¼ tsp
60 g (2½ oz)	chopped onion	40 g (1½ oz)
1 tbsp	olive oil	1 tbsp
3–4 tbsp	grated Parmesan cheese	4–5 tbsp

METHOD

Dice bacon. Fry until crisp. Drain and cool. Put bacon and next seven ingredients in bread tin in order suggested by your bread machine instructions. Set for dough. Press Start. While dough is rising, sauté onions in remaining olive oil. Set aside to cool.

When dough is ready, punch it down on a lightly floured board. Let it rest a few minutes. Gently knead in the onions. Then roll it into an oval, about 1 cm (½ inch) thick. With a sharp knife, make several diagonal cuts in the bread, and stretch the dough so the cuts open wide. Sprinkle cornmeal on a baking sheet. Put the dough on the sheet. Sprinkle with the cheese. Cover with lightly buttered greaseproof paper or clingfilm. Put in a warm place to rise for 45 minutes. Bake bread in a preheated 190°C/375°F/Gas 5 oven for about 20 to 25 minutes.

BRAIDED BRIOCHE

*This pretty plaited loaf uses a traditional brioche recipe, rich with eggs and butter.
It is full of flavour and good simply plain, but it can be buttered or used for toast.*

450 g (1 lb) LOAF	INGREDIENTS	675 g (1½ lb) LOAF
4 tbsp	milk	6 tbsp
2	eggs	3
6 tbsp	butter, at room temperature	125 g (4½ oz)
3 tbsp	sugar	4½ tbsp
½ tsp	salt	¾ tsp
270 g (10 oz)	bread flour	425 g (15 oz)
1½ tsp	yeast	2¼ tsp

TOPPING

1 egg yolk
1 tsp water
2–3 tbsp sliced almonds

METHOD

Put dough ingredients in bread tin in order suggested by your bread machine instructions. Set for dough. Press Start.

When dough is ready, punch it down on a lightly floured board. Let it rest a few minutes. Cut it into three pieces. Roll each piece to form a thin rope, about 40 cm (15 inches) long for the smaller loaf, 45 to 50 cm (18 to 20 inches) for the larger. Put the three ropes on a lightly buttered baking sheet. At one end, pinch the three ends together. Then plait loosely, pinching the ends together at the bottom. Make a wash of the egg yolk and water, lightly beating with a fork. Paint the wash on the top of the bread and sprinkle with the almonds.

Cover and let rise 45 to 60 minutes in a warm place. When bread has risen, place in a preheated 180°C/350°F/ Gas 4 oven and bake for about 30 to 50 minutes.

TUSCAN SAGE WHOLEWHEAT BREAD

Flavoured with fresh sage that has been sautéed in olive oil, this bread is delicious with game or roast meats.

450 g (1 lb) LOAF	INGREDIENTS	675 g (1½ lb) LOAF
12 leaves	fresh sage	18 leaves
2 tbsp	olive oil	3 tbsp
175 ml (6 fl oz)	water	250 ml (8 fl oz)
1 tbsp	sugar	1½ tbsp
1 tsp	salt	1½ tsp
95 g (3½ oz)	wholewheat flour	130 g (5 oz)
185 g (6½ oz)	bread flour	270 g (10 oz)
2 tsp	yeast	1 tbsp

TOPPING

1 egg, lightly beaten with a fork
2 tsp water
freshly crushed pepper

METHOD

Tear sage leaves into several pieces. Heat oil in small frying pan. Add sage to oil and sauté for 1 minute, removing from heat sooner if oil is too hot. Leaves must not be scorched. Let cool for 10 minutes. Put sage, oil and remaining dough ingredients in bread tin in order suggested by your bread machine instructions. Set for wholewheat bread, dough stage. Press Start.

When dough is ready, punch it down on a lightly floured board. Let it rest a few minutes. Sprinkle cornmeal on a baking sheet. Shape the dough into a round and put it on the baking sheet. Combine the egg and water and brush over the top of the dough. Sprinkle crushed pepper over top. Cover and let rise in a warm place for 1 hour.

With a sharp knife, make three slashes in the top of the bread. Place in a preheated 190°C/375°F/Gas 5 oven and bake until the top is golden brown, 30 to 45 minutes.

ITALIAN SAUSAGE BREAD

This bread is wrapped around a substantial filling of sausage, cheese, pine nuts and onion. It makes a great snack for watching football – or serve it with a vegetable soup or minestrone.

450 g (1 lb) LOAF	INGREDIENTS	675 g (1½ lb) LOAF
120 ml (4 fl oz)	milk	175 ml (6 fl oz)
4 tbsp	water	6 tbsp
1 tbsp	butter	1½ tbsp
1 tbsp	sugar	1½ tbsp
1 tsp	dried basil	1½ tsp
½ tsp	dried oregano	¾ tsp
1 tsp	salt	1½ tsp
270 g (10 oz)	bread flour	425 g (15 oz)
1½ tsp	yeast	2¼ tsp

	FILLING	
225 g (8 oz)	Italian sausage	350 g (12 oz)
25 g (1 oz)	finely chopped onion	40 g (1½ oz)
1	clove garlic, chopped	1 or 2
2 tbsp	pine kernels	3 tbsp
1	egg, lightly beaten	1
175 g (6 oz)	grated mozzarella	275 g (9 oz)

METHOD

Put dough ingredients in bread tin in order suggested by your bread machine instructions. Set for white bread, dough stage. Press Start.

While the dough is working, make the filling. Crumble the sausage into a hot frying pan and cook, stirring often, until sausage is browned. Drain and remove sausage. Chop the sausage into small bits. Discard all but 1 tablespoon of fat.

Reheat the fat and sauté onion, garlic and pine nuts for 5 minutes. Combine the onion mixture with the cooked sausage. When mixture has cooled slightly, add the egg and mix well.

When dough is ready, punch it down on a lightly floured board. Let it rest a few minutes. Butter a 25-cm (9½-inch) loaf tin. Roll the dough out into a rectangle no wider than the length of the bread tin. Gently spread the sausage filling over the surface of the bread, taking care not to tear the dough. Sprinkle the mozzarella over the filling. Starting at the short end, roll dough into a cylinder. If necessary, turn ends under. Put the dough into the bread tin, seam side down. Cover and let rise in a warm place for 1 hour.

Bake in a preheated 180°C/350°F/Gas 4 oven until golden, about 35 to 40 minutes. Let cool slightly, then slice and serve while warm.

TIP

If you use freshly grated cheese, pack it tightly or much of the measurement will be air.

BREADSTICKS, ROLLS AND QUICKBREADS

Walnut Cheese Breadsticks   112

Armenian Sesame Rolls   113

Pumpkin Cranberry Rolls   114

Rye Breadsticks with
Peppercorns   115

Rosemary Currant
Butter Rolls   115

Southern Feather Rolls   116

Wholewheat Sesame Rolls   116

Bialys   118

WALNUT CHEESE BREADSTICKS

*Toasting the walnuts boosts the flavour of these crisp breadsticks. Enjoy them with
a meal or snack or with a glass of red wine.*

MAKES 16–20	INGREDIENTS	MAKES 24–30
4 tbsp	finely chopped walnuts	6 tbsp
140 ml (5 fl oz)	water	200 ml (7 fl oz)
1 tbsp	sugar	1½ tbsp
2 tbsp	vegetable oil	3 tbsp
25 g (1 oz)	grated Cheddar cheese	40 g (1½ oz)
1 tsp	salt	1½ tsp
270 g (10 oz)	bread flour	425 g (15 oz)
1½ tsp	yeast	2¼ tsp

EGG WASH

1 egg white

2 tsp water

METHOD

Spread the walnuts on a small baking sheet and put in a preheated 180°C/350°F/Gas 4 oven for 7 to 12 minutes. Watch closely and stir often until walnuts turn a deeper brown and give off a toasty scent. Let cool.

Put cooled walnuts and remaining dough ingredients in bread tin in order suggested by your bread machine instructions. Set for white bread, dough stage. Press Start.

Grease two or three baking sheets.

When dough is ready, remove from bread tin and punch down. Cut smaller quantity into 16 to 20 pieces, larger into 24 to 30 pieces. Roll each piece between your palms to form a thin rope, about 15 to 20 cm (6 to 8 inches) long. Place breadsticks 2.5 cm (1 inch) apart on baking sheets. Cover loosely and put in a warm place to rise for 20 to 25 minutes.

Beat egg white and water together with a fork. Brush over breadsticks. Bake in a preheated 180°C/350°F/Gas 4 oven until golden brown, 20 to 25 minutes.

ARMENIAN SESAME ROLLS

The egg dough for these rolls is divided into ropes that are coiled into snails and sprinkled with sesame seeds. Baked to a golden brown, they are an impressive sight at breakfast, tea or dinner.

MAKES 8	INGREDIENTS	MAKES 12
1	egg	2
125 ml (4 fl oz)	milk	175 ml (6 fl oz)
2 tbsp	butter	3 tbsp
3 tbsp	sugar	4½ tbsp
½ tsp	salt	¾ tsp
270 g (10 oz)	bread flour	425 g (15 oz)
1½ tsp	yeast	2¼ tsp

TOPPING

1 egg, beaten with a fork
2–3 tbsp sesame seeds

METHOD

Put dough ingredients in the bread tin, adding them in the order suggested by your bread machine instructions.

Set for white bread, dough stage. Press Start.

When dough is ready, punch it down on a lightly floured board. Let it rest a few minutes. Sprinkle cornmeal on two baking sheets. Cut the dough into 8 pieces for the smaller recipe, 12 pieces for the larger. Roll each piece between your hands until it forms a long, thin rope, 20 to 25 cm (8 to 10 inches) long. Beginning at one end, coil the rope around itself like a snail, and pinch the end under the outside of the coil. Put the coils 5 cm (2 inches) apart on the baking sheets.

Brush the tops with the beaten egg and sprinkle generously with sesame seeds. Cover, put in a warm place and let rise 1½ to 2 hours.

Bake in a preheated 190°C/375°F/Gas 5 oven until the rolls are golden brown, 15 to 20 minutes.

PUMPKIN CRANBERRY ROLLS

These are great dinner rolls during the holidays or at any time. The pumpkin flavour is subtle, the dried cranberries add a nice tang and the rolls are not sweet. They are best served warm.

MAKES 12	INGREDIENTS	MAKES 18
175 ml (6 fl oz)	pumpkin purée	250 ml (8 fl oz)
1	egg	1 egg + 1 yolk
2 tbsp	powdered milk	3 tbsp
2 tbsp	butter	3 tbsp
2 tbsp	sugar	3 tbsp
1 tsp	salt	1½ tsp
½ tsp	cinnamon	¾ tsp
½ tsp	ground ginger	¾ tsp
¼ tsp	ground cloves	¼ tsp
270 g (10 oz)	bread flour	425 g (15 oz)
1½ tsp	yeast	2¼ tsp
40 g (1½ oz)	sweetened dried cranberries	55 g (2 oz)

METHOD

Put all ingredients except cranberries in bread tin in order suggested by your bread machine instructions. Set for white bread, dough stage. Press Start. After about 15 minutes or when the beeper signals time to add fruit, add the cranberries.

Butter muffin tins: 12 cups for the smaller recipe, 18 cups for the larger recipe.

When dough is ready, punch it down and let it rest a few minutes. Cut dough into 12 pieces for the smaller recipe, 18 pieces for the larger. Roll each piece into a ball; it does not have to be perfectly round. Place each ball of dough in a muffin cup. Set in a warm place to rise until doubled in size, 45 to 60 minutes.

When dough is ready, bake in a preheated 180°C/350°F/ Gas 4 oven until a knife or wooden pick inserted in the middle of a roll comes out clean, about 15 minutes.

RYE BREADSTICKS WITH PEPPERCORNS

Crushed pepper adds zip to these breadsticks, while rosemary – fresh or dried – adds flavour.

MAKES 16–20	INGREDIENTS	MAKES 24–30
175 ml (6 fl oz)	water	250 ml (8 fl oz)
1 tbsp	sugar	1½ tbsp
2 tbsp	vegetable oil	3 tbsp
2 tsp	finely chopped fresh rosemary	1 tbsp
1 tsp	crushed peppercorns	1½ tsp
1 tsp	salt	1½ tsp
95 g (3½ oz)	rye flour	130 g (5 oz)
185 g (6½ oz)	bread flour	270 g (10 oz)
1½ tsp	yeast	2¼ tsp

EGG WASH

1 egg white
2 tsp water

METHOD

Put dough ingredients in bread tin in order suggested by your bread machine instructions. Set for wholewheat bread, dough stage. Press Start.

Grease two or three baking sheets.

When dough is ready, remove from bread tin and punch down. Cut small quantity into 16 to 20 pieces, larger into 24 to 30 pieces. Roll each piece between your palms to form a thin rope, about 15 to 20 cm (6 to 8 inches) long. Place breadsticks 2.5 cm (1 inch) apart on baking sheets. Cover loosely and put in a warm place to rise for 20 to 25 minutes.

Beat egg white and water together with a fork. Brush over breadsticks. Bake in a preheated 180°C/350°F/Gas 4 oven until golden brown, 20 to 25 minutes.

ROSEMARY CURRANT BUTTER ROLLS

These buttery wholewheat dinner rolls demonstrate the surprisingly complementary flavours of currants and rosemary.

MAKES 8–10	INGREDIENTS	MAKES 12–15
1	egg	2
150 ml (5 fl oz)	milk	175 ml (6 fl oz)
1 tbsp	sugar	1½ tbsp
2 tbsp	butter	3 tbsp
2 tsp	finely chopped fresh rosemary	1 tbsp
1 tsp	salt	1½ tsp
95 g (3½ oz)	wholewheat flour	130 g (5 oz)
185 g (6½ oz)	bread flour	270 g (10 oz)
1½ tsp	yeast	2¼ tsp
50 g (2 oz)	currants	75 g (3 oz)
1½–2 tbsp	very soft butter	2–3 tbsp

METHOD

Put all ingredients except currants and soft butter in bread tin in order suggested by your bread machine instructions. Set for wholewheat bread, dough stage. Press Start. After about 15 minutes or when the beeper signals time to add fruit, add currants.

Butter muffin tins: 8 to 10 cups for the smaller recipe, 12 to 15 cups for the larger.

When dough is ready, punch it down on a floured board. Let it rest a few minutes. Roll into a rectangle 8 mm (⅓ inch) thick, squaring off the corners. Spread softened butter over surface. Cut the dough lengthwise into four strips. Stack the four strips, one on top of the other. Trim the uneven ends. Cut through the width of the stack, into 8 to 10 pieces for the smaller recipe, 12 to 15 pieces for the larger. Put each piece in a muffin cup. Cut edges up so that as they rise they will fan out slightly. Cover loosely and put in a warm place to rise for 1 hour. Bake in a preheated 180°C/350°F/Gas 4 oven for about 25 minutes.

SOUTHERN FEATHER ROLLS

These rolls come from the southern United States, where dinner rolls as light as a feather are the pride of many a table.

MAKES 12	INGREDIENTS	MAKES 18
1	egg	2
2 tbsp	water	3 tbsp
175 ml (6 fl oz)	milk	250 ml (8 fl oz)
3 tbsp	butter	4½ tbsp
2 tbsp	sugar	3 tbsp
1 tsp	salt	1½ tsp
270 g (10 oz)	bread flour	425 g (15 oz)
1½ tsp	yeast	2¼ tsp

METHOD

Put ingredients in bread tin in order suggested by your bread machine instructions. Set for dough stage. Press Start.

Butter muffin tins: 12 cups for the smaller recipe, 18 cups for the larger recipe.

When dough is ready, flour your hands. Remove dough from bread tin and place on floured surface. This dough is very soft and sticky. If your bread machine has not punched it down, knead dough lightly, just enough to press out air but incorporate as little additional flour as possible. Keeping your hands lightly floured, shape the dough into a fat log and cut into 12 equal pieces for the smaller recipe, 18 pieces for the larger.

Place each piece into a muffin cup. Put rolls in a warm place to rise for 40 minutes. Bake in a preheated 180°C/350°F/Gas 4 oven until tops are just lightly browned, 20 to 25 minutes.

WHOLEWHEAT SESAME ROLLS

These rolls are basic wholewheat rolls, made from a slightly stiff dough so the rounds hold their shape on the baking sheet.

MAKES 8	INGREDIENTS	MAKES 12
175 ml (6 fl oz)	water	250 ml (8 fl oz)
1 tbsp	vegetable oil	1½ tbsp
1 tbsp	sugar	1½ tbsp
1 tsp	salt	1½ tsp
130 g (5 oz)	bread flour	200g (7½ oz)
130 g (5 oz)	wholewheat flour	200g (7½ oz)
1½ tsp	yeast	2¼ tsp

TOPPING

2–3 tbsp milk
2–3 tbsp sesame seeds

METHOD

Put all dough ingredients in bread tin in order suggested by your bread machine instructions. Set for dough. Press Start.

When dough is ready, punch it down on a lightly floured board. Let it rest a few minutes, then take it between your hands and roll it into a thick log. Cut log into 8 equal pieces for the smaller recipe, 12 pieces for the larger recipe. Roll each piece into a ball, flatten slightly and put on one or two non-stick or lightly buttered baking sheets. Cover, put in a warm place and let rise for 1 hour.

When dough has risen, brush lightly with milk and sprinkle with sesame seeds. Cut a cross in the top of each. Bake in a preheated 190°C/375°F/Gas 5 oven until light brown, 15 to 18 minutes.

RIGHT Wholewheat Sesame Rolls

BIALYS

*These are Polish rolls, related to bagels, with an onion and poppy seed filling. The
dough should be allowed to rise three times instead of the usual two.*

MAKES 8	INGREDIENTS	MAKES 12
175 ml (6 fl oz)	water	275 ml (9 fl oz)
2 tsp	sugar	1 tbsp
1 tsp	salt	1½ tsp
270 g (10 oz)	bread flour	425 g (15 oz)
1½ tsp	yeast	2¼ tsp
	FILLING	
25 g (1 oz)	finely chopped onion	40 g (1½ oz)
2 tsp	poppy seeds	1 tbsp
1 tbsp	vegetable oil	1½ tbsp
¼ tsp	salt	½ tsp

METHOD

Put dough ingredients in bread tin in order suggested by
your bread machine instructions. Set for white bread,
dough stage. Press Start.

While dough is in bread machine, make filling by
combining all ingredients.

When dough is ready, remove from bread machine and
punch down. Put it in a buttered bowl and turn so all
sides of dough are buttered. Cover and put in a warm
place to rise for 40 minutes.

Punch down again. Cut smaller recipe into 8 equal
pieces, larger recipe into 12 pieces. Roll each piece into
a ball and flatten. Place rolls on a baking sheet that has
been sprinkled with cornmeal. Make a 5-cm (1-inch)
indentation in the centre of each roll (the bottom of a
shot glass works well).

Cover with lightly buttered greaseproof paper or cling
film. Put in a warm place to rise for 30 minutes. If the
indentations have filled in, indent again. Put some of
the filling in each indentation, dividing filling equally
among all the rolls.

Bake in a preheated 230°C/450°F/Gas 8 oven until
lightly browned, about 20 minutes.

HOLIDAY BREADS

Alsatian Christmas Bread   120

Apricot Almond Babka   121

Moravian Sugar Rolls   122

Greek Easter Bread   123

Barm Brack   124

Cherry Christmas Wreath   126

Italian Christmas Roll   127

ALSATIAN CHRISTMAS BREAD

This bread from the Alsace region of France is very different because it uses only enough brioche dough to hold a large quantity and variety of dried fruit together in a loaf. It is best when made with many different fruits – I use nine when I make it – but the selection can be varied. The fruit is marinated in Kirsch overnight. Although related to fruit cake, it uses a yeast dough and does not call for bitter ingredients such as candied peel that are traditional in fruit cake. The bread is traditionally served on Christmas Eve, or with breakfast on Christmas and New Year's Day. This is a sweet, dense bread that should be eaten in thin slices and does not need butter. Because the loaf uses such a small amount of bread dough, it does not matter what size machine tin you use.

FRUIT

A total of 550 g (1 lb 4 oz) of any combination
of the following chopped fruits:
dried apples, figs, sultanas, dried
sweet cherries, dried apricots, dried peaches,
dates, dried pears, dried cranberries, dried
pineapple, dried mango
250 ml (8 fl oz) Kirsch or cherry-flavoured brandy
$\frac{1}{2}$ tsp cinnamon
2 tbsp plain or bread flour
100 g (4 oz) chopped walnuts

BRIOCHE DOUGH

2 tbsp milk
1 egg
3 tbsp butter, at room temperature
1 tbsp sugar
$\frac{1}{4}$ tsp salt
130 g (5 oz) bread flour
$\frac{3}{4}$ tsp yeast

METHOD

The night before you make this bread, mix the fruits, Kirsch and cinnamon and let marinate.

The following day, put brioche ingredients in bread tin in order suggested by your bread machine instructions. Set for white bread, dough stage. Press Start.

While dough is working, drain the fruit well and discard the Kirsch. Mix the flour with the fruit, then stir in the walnuts. Lightly butter a loaf tin that is 20 to 25 cm (8 to 9½ inches) long.

When dough is ready, punch it down on a lightly floured board. Let it rest a few minutes. Put the dough in a large mixing bowl and mix in the fruit. As you do this, the dough will tear into bits. Shape the mixture into a loaf and place in buttered loaf tin.

Cover and put in a warm place for 45 minutes. You will not see a lot of rising. Place bread in a preheated 190°C/375°F/Gas 5 oven and bake for 40 minutes.

Apricot Almond Babka

Babka is a Polish holiday bread, related to brioche, rich with butter and eggs. Because of the high amount of butter and liquids, it will not bake properly in the bread machine and must be baked in the oven in a brioche tin, 25-cm (10-inch) Bundt tin or tube tin. Because of the type of tin that must be used, only a recipe for a 680-g (1½-pound) loaf is given.

INGREDIENTS

125 ml (4 fl oz) milk

3 eggs

8 tbsp butter at room temperature

70 g (2½ oz) sugar

1 tsp salt

1½ tsp vanilla extract

425 g (15 oz) bread flour

2¼ tsp yeast

50 g (2 oz) chopped dried apricots

20 g (¾ oz) slivered almonds

3 tsp icing sugar

METHOD

Put first eight ingredients in bread tin in order suggested by your bread machine instructions. Set for white bread, dough stage. Press Start. After about 15 minutes add apricots and almonds.

Butter the tin. If your bread machine has not punched down the dough, gently work it between your hands and squeeze out air. This is a very wet, sticky dough – almost a batter – which cannot be kneaded in the usual way; no flour should be added. Put the dough in the baking tin and spread so it makes an even circle.

Cover with lightly buttered greaseproof paper or clingfilm. Put in a warm place and let rise until doubled in size, about 40 minutes.

Bake in a preheated 190°C/375°F/Gas 5 oven, 30 to 35 minutes in a Bundt or tube tin, 45 to 55 minutes in a brioche tin. Test by sticking a knife in a deep spot in the bread. If it comes out clean, bread is ready. Cool on a wire rack, and sprinkle the sugar over the top.

MORAVIAN SUGAR ROLLS

These sweet rolls with a sugary walnut topping come from the Moravians, a religious group that emigrated from Czechoslovakia and settled in Pennsylvania and North Carolina.

MAKES 12	INGREDIENTS	MAKES 18
50 ml (2 fl oz)	water	50 ml (2 fl oz)
2 tbsp	powdered milk	3 tbsp
1	egg	2
65 g (2½ oz)	mashed potatoes	95 g (3¾ oz)
4 tbsp	butter	6 tbsp
3 tbsp	honey	4½ tbsp
1 tsp	vanilla extract	1½ tsp
1 tsp	cinnamon	1½ tsp
½ tsp	salt	¾ tsp
300 g (11 oz)	bread flour	425 g (15 oz)
1½ tsp	yeast	2¼ tsp

TOPPING

MAKES 12	INGREDIENTS	MAKES 18
2 tbsp	very soft butter	3 tbsp
4 tbsp	brown sugar	6 tbsp
½ tsp	cinnamon	¾ tsp
pinch	ground nutmeg	¼ tsp
4 tbsp	chopped walnuts	6 tbsp

METHOD

Put dough ingredients in bread tin in order suggested by your bread machine instructions. Set for white bread, dough stage. Press Start.

Butter muffin tins: 12 cups for the smaller recipe, 18 cups for the larger recipe. Make the topping by using a fork to mash together the butter, brown sugar and spices. Stir in the walnuts.

When dough is ready, turn out onto a lightly floured board and punch down. Roll into a rope. Cut smaller quantity into 12 equal pieces, larger into 18 pieces. Roll each piece into a ball – it does not have to be perfectly round – and put into a muffin cup. Turn so all sides are buttered. Spread some of the topping on each ball of dough.

Put in a warm place to rise for 1 hour. Bake in a preheated 180°C/350°F/Gas 4 oven until dough is golden, 20 to 25 minutes.

NOTE

This recipe is based on pure mashed potatoes with no additions. If milk or other liquids have been added to the potatoes, check during kneading and add a little flour if dough is too wet.

GREEK EASTER BREAD

This plaited bread is made from a sweet egg dough flavoured with lemon, vanilla and aniseed, but what sets it apart from other breads is the eggs, which are tucked whole into the plait and baked with the bread. If you wish, you may sprinkle 2 to 3 tablespoons of sesame seeds over the bread before baking.

450 g (1 lb) LOAF	INGREDIENTS	675 g (1½ lb) LOAF
1	egg	2
65 ml (2½ fl oz)	milk	65 ml (2½ fl oz)
1 tbsp	water	2 tbsp
32 g (2¼ oz)	sugar	80 g (3¼ oz)
4 tbsp	butter	6 tbsp
1 tsp	grated lemon zest	1½ tsp
1 tsp	vanilla extract	1½ tsp
1 tsp	aniseed, preferably crushed	1½ tsp
1 tsp	salt	1½ tsp
270 g (10 oz)	bread flour	425 g (15 oz)
1½ tsp	yeast	2¼ tsp
4 tbsp	sultanas	6 tbsp
2–3	whole eggs, uncooked	4–5

EGG WASH

1 egg, beaten with a fork

2 tsp milk

METHOD

Put all dough ingredients except sultanas and whole eggs in bread tin in order suggested by your bread machine instructions. Set for dough stage. Press Start. After about 15 minutes or when the beeper signals time to add fruit, add sultanas.

When dough is ready, punch it down on a lightly floured board. Let it rest a few minutes. Then cut it into three equal pieces. Take each piece between your hands and roll it into a rope, about 30 to 35 cm (12 to 14 inches) long for the smaller loaf, 40 to 45 cm (15 to 18 inches) for the larger. Lay the three ropes on a non-stick or lightly buttered baking sheet. Beginning at one end, pinch the ends together and plait the three ropes, then pinch the bottom ends together. Bring the ends around to make a circle. Carefully ease the whole eggs between strands of dough.

Combine the egg and milk and brush it over the bread. Cover and let rise until bread has doubled in bulk, 45 to 60 minutes.

Place in a preheated 190°C/375°F/Gas 5 oven and bake until the top is golden brown, about 30 to 35 minutes.

BARM BRACK

Barm Brack is an Irish fruit bread, eaten on St Brigid's feast day, February 1. This is a heavy, sweet bread which tends to scorch when baked in the bread machine because of the high sugar content. It should be baked in the oven.

450 g (1 lb) LOAF	INGREDIENTS	675 g (1½ lb) LOAF
1	egg	2
125 ml (4 fl oz)	milk	175 ml (6 fl oz)
2 tbsp	butter	3 tbsp
3 tbsp	brown sugar	4½ tbsp
¼ tsp	cinnamon	½ tsp
¼ tsp	ground nutmeg	½ tsp
½ tsp	salt	¾ tsp
270 g (10 oz)	bread flour	425 g (15 oz)
2 tsp	yeast	1 tbsp
3 tbsp	candied orange peel	4½ tbsp
35 g (1½ oz)	sultanas	50 g (2 oz)

METHOD

Put all ingredients except orange peel and sultanas in bread tin in order suggested by your bread machine instructions. Set for dough. Press Start. After about 15 minutes or when the beeper signals time to add fruit, add orange and raisins.

When dough is ready, punch it down on a lightly floured board. Let it rest a few minutes. Butter a 25-cm (9½-inch) loaf tin (can be smaller for smaller loaf). Shape the dough into a loaf and put it in the pan, turning so all sides are buttered. Cover and let rise in a warm place for 1 hour.

When bread has risen, bake in a preheated 180°C/350°F/ Gas 4 oven until the top is golden, about 30 to 45 minutes.

CHERRY CHRISTMAS WREATH

This holiday bread is made with a sweet, buttery dough that is flavoured with orange zest, vanilla, spices and dried cherries, then formed into a circle.

450 g (1 lb) LOAF	INGREDIENTS	675 g (1½ lb) LOAF
1	egg	1 + 1 yolk
7 tbsp	milk	175 ml (6 fl oz)
3 tbsp	butter	4½ tbsp
3 tbsp	sugar	4½ tbsp
½ tsp	salt	¾ tsp
1 tsp	grated orange zest	1½ tsp
½ tsp	ground ginger	¾ tsp
1 tsp	ground nutmeg	1½ tsp
1 tsp	vanilla extract	1½ tsp
270 g (10 oz)	bread flour	425 g (15 oz)
1½ tsp	yeast	2¼ tsp
50 g (2 oz)	dried sweet cherries	75 g (3 oz)
2 tbsp	sliced almonds	3 tbsp
1–2 tbsp	icing sugar	2–3 tbsp

METHOD

Put all ingredients except cherries, almonds and icing sugar in bread tin in order suggested by your bread machine instructions. Set for white bread, dough stage. Press Start. After about 15 minutes or when the beeper signals time to add fruit, add cherries.

When dough is ready, punch it down on a lightly floured board. Let it rest a few minutes, then take it between your hands and roll it into a rope, about 40 cm (15 inches) long for the smaller loaf, 45 to 50 cm (18 to 20 inches) for the larger. Put it on a non-stick or lightly buttered baking sheet. Bring the ends together to form a circle. Make diagonal cuts around the outside of the bread to resemble the points of leaves. Sprinkle almonds over dough and press lightly.

Cover and let rise for 45 to 60 minutes. Bake in a preheated 180°C/350°F/Gas 4 oven until golden, about 30 to 40 minutes. Remove from oven and sprinkle with icing sugar.

ITALIAN CHRISTMAS ROLL

Filled with fruit and nuts, this sweet loaf is from the Naples area, and is known in Italy as Rotolo di Natale. If you wish, you may adopt a modern tradition and mix one tablespoon of unsweetened cocoa with the fruit mixture. Brandy or rum can be substituted for the Marsala wine.

450 g (1 lb) LOAF	INGREDIENTS	675 g (1½ lb) LOAF
	FILLING	
50 g (2 oz)	chopped figs	75 g (3 oz)
65 g (2½ oz)	chopped dried apples	100 g (4 oz)
40 g (1½ oz)	sultanas	60 g (2¼ oz)
3 tbsp	sugar	4½ tbsp
3 tbsp	Marsala wine	4½ tbsp
1–2 tbsp	very soft butter	2–3 tbsp
40 g (1½ oz)	chopped walnuts	60 g (2¼ oz)
4 tbsp	pine kernels	6 tbsp
	BREAD	
1	egg	2
120 ml (4 fl oz)	milk	190 ml (6½ fl oz)
3 tbsp	butter	4½ tbsp
4 tbsp	sugar	6 tbsp
1 tsp	grated lemon zest	1½ tsp
1 tsp	almond extract	1½ tsp
1 tsp	salt	1½ tsp
300 g (11 oz)	bread flour	425 g (15 oz)
1½ tsp	yeast	2¼ tsp

TOPPING

1 egg, lightly beaten with 2 tsp water
1–2 tbsp sugar

METHOD

Preferably the night before baking, or at least several hours before, mix the fruits, sugar and Marsala wine for the filling. Stir well and let marinate.

The next day, put dough ingredients in bread tin in order suggested by your bread machine instructions. Set for dough stage. Press Start.

Drain any liquid off the fruit and discard.

When dough is ready, punch it down on a lightly floured board. Let it rest a few minutes, then roll it out into a rectangle about 25 x 40 cm (10 x 15 inches) for the smaller loaf, about 40 x 40 cm (15 x 15 inches) for the larger one. Spread the soft butter over the dough. Spread the drained fruit over the butter, then sprinkle walnuts and pine kernels over fruit.

Starting at a long end, roll the dough into a tight cylinder. Place the roll on a buttered baking sheet and pull ends together to form a circle. Cover, put in a warm place and let rise until doubled in bulk, about 1 hour.

Brush with egg wash and sprinkle with sugar. Bake in a preheated 190°C/375°F/Gas 5 oven until brown, 25 to 40 minutes.

Alsatian Christmas bread 120
Anadama bread 82
Apple: apple-cranberry Graham
    bread 84
    applesauce oat bran bread 75
    braid 95
    pecan bread, sweet potato 80
Apricot: almond babka 121
    pecan anadama bread 82
    Scandinavian tea ring 98
Armenium sesame rolls 113

Babka, apricot almond 121
Banana nut cinnamon swirl 93
Barm Brack 124
Bialys 118
Bran bread: applesauce oat
    bran 75
    cinnamon-orange 42
    crunchy 36
    pineapple orange 77
Breadsticks 112, 115
Brioche, braided 107
Buttermilk bread: chive 28
    multi-grain 34

California fruit braid 91
Carrot ginger wholewheat bread
    70
Cheese bread: coriander pesto
    103
    foccacio with olives and
        sun-dried tomatoes 102
    fougasse 106
    herbed cottage cheese 22
    Italian sausage bread 110
    jalapeño 72
    Kathy's pepper 27
    onion 73
    savoury kugelhopf 104
    spinach cheese swirl 101
    walnut cheese breadsticks
        112
    walnut ricotta wholewheat 27
Cherry Christmas wreath 126
Christmas breads 120, 126
Cinnamon: apple braid 95
    orange bran bread 42
    swirl, banana nut 93
Coconut date bread 77
Corn rye bread 44
Coriander pesto bread 103
Courgette 83
Cranberry: apple Graham bread
    84
    rolls, pumpkin 114
Cuban bread with yuca 75

Dates 91
    date coconut bread 77
    date walnut pastries 87
    date-nut wheat bread 81

Easter bread 123

Foccacio: with olives and sun-

dried tomatoes 102
    wholewheat pesto 105
Fougasse 106
Fruit braid 91

Graham bread 67, 84
Grape-nut bread 39
Greek Easter bread 123

Herbs: herbed cottage cheese
    bread 22
    herbed wholewheat bread 40
    potato rye with caraway and
        dill 52
    sour cream wholewheat
        bread with herbs 24
    sourdough rosemary bread
        with olives 58

Italian Christmas roll 126
Italian sausage bread 110

Kugelhopf, savoury 104

Low-country beer bread with
    brown rice 40

Moravian sugar rolls 122
Multi-grain bread 31, 34

Norwegian cardamom bread 94

Oatmeal bread: with ginger and
    toasted almonds 33
    raisin 76
    wholewheat 32
    yoghurt 30
Onion: cheese bread 73
    dill onion yoghurt bread 25
    rye bread, with semolina 51

Pear wholewheat bread 78
Pepper cheese bread 27
Pineapple orange bran bread 77
Polentaporter bread 20
Potato bread 22, 88, 101, 122
    roasted garlic, with 68
    rye, with caraway and dill 52
    wholewheat sesame 33
Prune yoghurt breakfast
    crescents 99
Pumpkin: cranberry rolls 114
    Graham bread 67

Raisin bread: apple braid 95
    Barm Brack 124
    cinnamon raisin rolls 88
    Greek Easter 123
    Norwegian cardamom 94
    oatmeal 76
    pecan rye 46
    sourdough rye 56
    Tuscan sweet bread 89
Ricotta walnut wholewheat
    bread 27
Rolls: Armenium sesame 113

bialys 118
    cinnamon raisin 88
    Moravian sugar 122
    pumpkin cranberry 114
    rosemary currant butter 115
    Southern feather 116
    wholewheat sesame 116
Rye bread 44
    breadsticks with cracked
        rye 115
    corn 44
    dark 45
    dark and fruity 51
    double 46
    onion, with semolina 51
    potato, with caraway and
        dill 52
    raisin pecan 46
    Sisteron 64
    sourdough raisin 56
    sourdough seed 65
    Swedish 49
    wholewheat 48

Sage wholewheat bread,
    Tuscan 109
Sausage bread, Italian 110
Scandinavian tea ring with
    apricot cheese filling 98
Seed bread 36, 65
Semolina: bread with courgette
    and millet 83
    onion rye bread with 51
Sisteron rye bread 64
Soured cream: spiced bread 21
    wholewheat bread with
        herbs 24
Sourdough bread 55
    roasted garlic and peppers,
        with 57
    rosemary, with olives 58
    rye raisin 56
    rye seed 65
    Sisteron rye 64
    sourdough starter 54
    Southwestern spiced 63
    wholewheat, with bulgur
        61
    wholewheat, with sun-dried
        tomatoes 60
Southern feather rolls 116
Spinach cheese swirl 101
Swedish rye bread 49
Sweet potato: apple pecan
    bread 80
    wholewheat bread 71

Tomatoes, sun-dried 60, 102
Tuscan sage wholewheat bread
    109
Tuscan sweet bread 89

Walnut-date pastries 87
White bread 19
Wholewheat bread 20
    carrot ginger 70

with egg and honey 37
    herbed 40
    oatmeal 32
    pear 78
    pesto foccacio 105
    potato sesame 33
    rye 48
    sesame rolls 116
    soured cream, with herbs 24
    sourdough, with bulgur 61
    sourdough, with sun-dried
        tomatoes 60
    sweet potato 71
    Tuscan sage 109
    walnut ricotta 27
Wild rice bread 34

Yuca, Cuban bread with 75

Zeppoles (zappla) 92

Bread-making ingredients are
available by mail order from the
following suppliers.

Cook's Delight
360-364 High Street
Berkhamsted
Herts HP4 1HU
Ph 44 1442 863584;
Fax 44 1442 863702; email:
cooksd@global.net.co.uk
http://www.cooksdelight.co.uk

King Arthur Flour
P. O. Box 876
Norwich,
VT 05055-0876
Ph: 1 800 827 6836;
Fax 1 800 343 3002;
email: info@kingarthurflour.com;
http://www.kingarthurflour.com;